Deconstruction and the Spirit

Deconstruction and the Spirit

How Pastors Can Better Understand
Deconstruction and How to Approach
It from a Pentecostal Perspective

Esteban Solís

WIPF & STOCK · Eugene, Oregon

DECONSTRUCTION AND THE SPIRIT
How Pastors Can Better Understand Deconstruction and How to Approach It from a Pentecostal Perspective

Copyright © 2024 Esteban Solís. All rights reserved. Except for brief quotations in critical publications or reviews, no part of this book may be reproduced in any manner without prior written permission from the publisher. Write: Permissions, Wipf and Stock Publishers, 199 W. 8th Ave., Suite 3, Eugene, OR 97401.

Wipf & Stock
An Imprint of Wipf and Stock Publishers
199 W. 8th Ave., Suite 3
Eugene, OR 97401

www.wipfandstock.com

PAPERBACK ISBN: 979-8-3852-0127-3
HARDCOVER ISBN: 979-8-3852-0128-0
EBOOK ISBN: 979-8-3852-0129-7

VERSION NUMBER 02/20/24

Scripture quotations marked (NIV) are taken from the Holy Bible, New International Version®, NIV®. Copyright © 1973, 1978, 1984, 2011 by Biblica, Inc.™ Used by permission of Zondervan. All rights reserved worldwide. www.zondervan.com The "NIV" and "New International Version" are trademarks registered in the United States Patent and Trademark Office by Biblica, Inc.™

Scripture quotations marked (CEV) are from the Contemporary English Version Copyright © 1991, 1992, 1995 by American Bible Society. Used by Permission.

To my wife, Cristina, and my children Matías and Valeria; their love inspires my life.

To the amazing Iglesia El Centro, where Cris and I have learned how to be pastors.

To every pastor in need of direction, God is with you.

Contents

1 Postmodernism and the Global South | 1
2 Deconstruction Happens | 13
3 Deconstruction Happens from Inside | 21
4 Deconstruction Is Not a Method | 33
5 Deconstruction Is a Call | 46
6 Deconstruction Is a "Yes" to the Other | 55
7 Deconstruction Is Affirmative of Institutions . . . Is Not Destruction | 66
8 What Is Going On? The Descriptive Empirical Task | 75
9 Why Is This Going On? The Interpretive Task | 81
10 What Ought to Be Going On? The Normative Task | 89
11 How Might We Respond? The Pragmatic Task | 100

A Word of Advice | 124
Bibliography | 127

1

Postmodernism and the Global South[1]

THE EFFECTS OF MODERNISM and postmodernism in the Global South have been uneven. Different populations have had different degrees of exposure to them. González and González argue that "neither Latin America nor its various forms of Christianity were ever really modern."[2] If this is true, rapid changes in the region will force Latin Americans to leap from a nonmodern world straight to a postmodern one. Yet, Samuel Escobar recognizes the pluriform experience of Latin America not only because of the influence of media and technology, but also missionaries who, by means of evangelization and church planting among pockets of premodern cultures in the region, "are also carriers of modernity."[3] Modern attributes can be found in Latin America throughout all

1. There is a difference between postmodernism and postmodernity. Postmodernism refers to an intellectual movement, while postmodernity points to cultural phenomena. In general, I will use the terms interchangeably to refer to the current age the Western world (and other regions) face. See Smith, *Who's Afraid of Postmodernism*, 20.

2. González and González, *Christianity in Latin America*, 301.

3. Escobar, *New Global Mission*, 71.

social classes, especially in the capital cities which are also leaning towards postmodernity.

When it comes to my own country, Costa Rica, it is impossible to say it has been isolated from the effects of modernity. The high levels of literacy the country has had for decades, the widespread communication networks, the presence of European and North American Protestantism for more than a century, and the constant business exchange with foreigners have exposed the general population to the influences of Western ideas and ideals for a long time. Costa Ricans in general have assimilated modern thought and are now embracing a postmodern understanding of the world too. Most Latin American major cities probably share the same experience.

But what is postmodernism? For Argentinian author Lucas Magnin it is a sort of disenchanting sentiment towards what was before and uncertainty about what is to come. He points out *postmodernity* is the name Jean-François Lyotard gave to what Bauman called *liquid modernity*, Lipovetski *hypermodernity*, and Beck *second modernity*; its Eurocentric emphasis has led non-European authors to approach the subject with categories such as *postcolonialism, peripheric modernity,* and others.[4] Lyotard famously defined his term as "incredulity about meta-narratives,"[5] John Caputo clarifies Lyotard's definition does not mean these narratives are "definitely false, just not believable."[6]

Postmodernity can be experienced as a cultural mood or as a philosophical endeavor. Olson explains that *postmodernity as a cultural mood* manifests as skepticism about grand claims to truth, questioning "authority just because it is authority, tradition just because it is tradition and truth claims just because they are

---

4. Magnin, *Cristianismo y Posmodernidad*, 24. It is important to note that even when categories such as postcolonialism and postmodernism are both responses to the failures of modernity, such relation does not imply the terms are equivalent. The main difference, as noted, being the Eurocentric character of postmodernism, which will lead to different conclusions as will become apparent in the development of the present work.

5. Lyotard, *Postmodern Condition*, xxiii–xxiv.

6. Caputo, *Folly of God*, 73–74.

truth claims,"[7] that it tends towards destruction and too often becomes "a lazy excuse for radical individualism."[8] *Postmodernity as philosophical endeavor*, on the other hand, "constitutes a serious disenchantment with modernity and determination to find something to replace it without tossing aside all of the Enlightenment's achievements."[9] So even when there is a sense of discontinuity because of this disenchantment, there is also a sense of continuity with what was before (modernity). This leads Crystal Downing to define postmodernism simply as that which "follows the teachings of modernism," in the sense that it supersedes the modern by questioning its truth.[10] Perhaps that is why John Caputo finds the term *post-structuralism* more appropriate than postmodernism, because it clarifies what was going through the minds of the thinkers who championed this movement, he explains:

> The Structuralists argued that a system like language (and "culture" at large) is ruled by a deep grammar (structures), which runs beneath the variations in the rules of grammar in the natural languages. These structures see to it that everything that happens in language is governed by a rule, or "programmed," literally written in advance. This deep grammar was called *langue* (let's say the structure of language), as opposed to individual empirical utterances called *parole*, or "events" (let's say speech acts), which occur under the rule of these laws. The Post-Structuralists—the "Sixty-eighters" (*les Soixante-huitaires*), as in 1968—resisted this and argued for a more unruly unprogrammability, a good example is the metaphor—putting an optimal pressure on the rules in order to produce a novel and unpredictable effect—which is what they meant by "events." Derrida produced the central document in this debate, which was very appropriately entitled *Of Grammatology*, meaning that

---

7. Olson, *Journey of Modern Theology*, 652.
8. Olson, *Journey of Modern Theology*, 653.
9. Olson, *Journey of Modern Theology*, 653.
10. Downing, *How Postmodernism Serves (My) Faith*, 20.

the *logos* of *gramme* (trace) is an open-ended *logos* not a closed one, not a *pro-gramme*.[11]

Vanhoozer explains more succinctly that what post-structuralist or postmodern thought rejects are the following modern postulates: "(1) that reason is absolute and universal, (2) that individuals are autonomous, able to transcend their place in history, class, and culture, (3) that universal principles and procedures are objective whereas preferences are subjective."[12] So even when the postmodern or post-structuralist is trying to find new ways to deal with the realities of life, it honestly acknowledges its roots and origins tracing them back to modernity.

Perhaps we could see modernity and postmodernity as a story of misplaced hopes. Modernity placed its hope heavily on human reason and inaugurated a new era of democracies, education, and unparalleled scientific accomplishments. Postmodernity recognizes the unquestionable achievements of modernity, but it is also unwilling to deny the general disenchantment in the midst of the totalizing godlike attitudes of modernity and the appalling moral failures of modern societies; no matter how far we got, it was never enough to fulfill humankind's deepest longings.

So, modernity began out of a deification of human reason, while postmodernity started out of disenchantment with this idol. At this point faith finds an ally since "Christianity and postmodernism share a concern to tear down idols."[13] There is much in postmodernity that Christianity can take advantage of; nevertheless, we should never forget that the foundation of postmodern thinking is a disenchantment with a misplaced hope. A Christian posture towards postmodernity should remain critical,[14] acknowledging

---

11. Caputo, *Folly of God*, 27.
12. Vanhoozer, *Cambridge Companion*, 8.
13. Olson, *Journey of Modern Theology*, 655.
14. Alan Padgett categorizes Christian responses to postmodernism in one of four self-explanatory categories: the ostrich, the bogeyman, the best buddy, and the critical dialogue partner. In Padgett, "Christianity and Postmodernity," 129.

the influence both modernity[15] and postmodernity have had on Christian theology and ultimately on Christian believers.

Two broad categories of Christian theologians have used a postmodern approach to theology in order to counter the effects of modernism in theology: postliberals and deconstructionists.

Postliberalism

Postliberals use narrative, tradition, community, and practice in an attempt to free Christianity from modern influences and transcend "liberalism ... and the left-middle-right spectrum of modern theology."[16] For Olson, Stanley Hauerwas, and William Willimon present postliberal theology more as a *mood* than a movement:

> We are no longer content . . . to stand on the periphery, hat in hand, apologetically trying to translate our religious convictions into terms palatable to the world. Rather, we are now ready to say that our convictions lay down a program, a vision, a paradigm for accommodating the world to the gospel. . . . There is an aggressive, anti-establishment spirit among [postliberals] that we think is right. That is, they challenge both the academy and the church to realize that business as usual cannot continue if Christians are to be intellectually and socially of service in our time.[17]

Postliberalism sees the Bible as "a realistic narrative that, in spite of flaws, conveys a picture of reality that serves as the lens through which Christians view reality . . . [freely admitting that the Bible] may be history-like without being historical."[18]

---

15. Nancey Murphy asserts that both conservative theologians (building upon Scripture) and liberal theologians (building upon experience) depend on modern assumptions and methods, but she believes postmodernism can provide a way between liberalism and Fundamentalism. In Murphy, *Beyond Liberalism and Fundamentalism*, 12.

16. Olson, *Journey of Modern Theology*, 656.

17. Hauerwas and Willimon, "Embarrassed by God's Presence," 98.

18. Olson, *Journey of Modern Theology*, 660–1.

Another important feature of this mood is that Christianity's primary language is worship and witness, while doctrine is conceived as second-order language functioning in a "regulative, not constitutive"[19] manner, seeing it more as ministerial (on a servant posture) than magisterial.[20]

An important use of witness involves Hauerwas's perspective on Christian apologetics which always lets modernity set the rules by assuming "the Christian God does not exist in order to work their way back to believing in God on the basis of entirely secular premises";[21] which is why from a postliberal perspective Christian communication towards society should be more about witnessing than assuming an apologetical stance.

Deconstructionism

The second branch of postmodern theology is deconstructive theology, which focuses on "commitment to the 'other' and critical exposure of the violent tendencies in all thought systems to move theology away from ideological idolatry toward openness to the new, the different and the unexpected."[22]

What Hauerwas is to postliberal theology, John Caputo is to deconstructive theology. Notable for moving from the field of philosophy to Christian theology, Caputo enacted with this transition the deconstructionist mood: whatever lines modernity drew are nothing but an invitation for those boundaries to be transgressed, for anything that has been constructed can be deconstructed. The postmodern impulse for transgressing boundaries might simply be a hypermodern manifestation of free will and autonomy, yet it shows the deconstructive mood and how the postmodern showcases both continuity and discontinuity of modern postures. One of the important discontinuities with modernity is the role of

---

19. Olson, *Journey of Modern Theology*, 661.
20. Olson, *Journey of Modern Theology*, 663.
21. Olson, *Journey of Modern Theology*, 664.
22. Olson, *Journey of Modern Theology*, 656.

religion. Caputo finds that both postmodernity and premodernity share an "openness to the sacred, to transcendence, to religion,"[23] quite an anti-modern posture.

Regarding the kingdom of God and the church, Olson thinks Caputo and Hauerwas would agree with Kierkegaard's portrayal of Christianity as standing in permanent structural opposition to this world; therefore, a sign of its decadence would be to sit at the table with that which it was called to stand in opposition to.[24] Nevertheless, Caputo and Hauerwas differ profoundly in their conception of the church which Caputo simply sees as the apostles' "Plan B"[25] when Jesus failed to return as expected, making it nothing more than a provisional construction. Olson concludes, "Caputo leaves no positive place for the church in his theology. It is just another human institution needing deconstruction and transformation. Hauerwas would agree that the church is not the kingdom of God and that every church needs improvement, but he would shudder at Caputo's cavalier treatment of the Church as if it were a mere afterthought of the apostles when Jesus did not return as expected."[26] So, along with Derrida (the father of deconstruction), Caputo shows strong reservations toward communities because of their "inbuilt tendency to become totalizing and exclusive."[27] Communities set protective boundaries around them, which deconstructionists tend to upset; as a community and an institution the idea of the church does not go very well with deconstructionism.

Now, we turn to a brief history of the concept of deconstruction. The "genealogy" of the French word *déconstruction* can be traced back across five languages to an unexpected but familiar source.[28] We find God getting tired of dealing with a people whose religious life was a superfluous repetition of human constructions,

---

23. Olson, *Journey of Modern Theology*, 696.
24. Olson, *Journey of Modern Theology*, 700.
25. Caputo, *What Would Jesus Deconstruct?*, 35.
26. Olson, *Journey of Modern Theology*, 707.
27. Olson, *Journey of Modern Theology*, 707.
28. Caputo, *Deconstruction in a Nutshell*, lvii.

a poor imitation of worship that lacked any substance. So, YHWH announced to the prophet:

> So once again I will do things that shock and amaze them, and I will destroy the wisdom of those who claim to know and understand. (Isa 29:14 CEV)

These human constructions resulted in the barren practice of hypocritical religion leading to estrangement of those who YHWH used to refer to as "my people," now plainly regarded as "this people." The once pious faith deteriorated into a "manipulative style of religion typical of paganism,"[29] relegating the central relationship with the Creator to the periphery of life. Once this happens, attention to the words spoken by God's prophets is neglected, in times of crisis the leaders instead choose to trust "their own wise and 'realistic' plans"[30] which end up threatening the future as announced by God. The ineludible conclusion then, is that such human wit must perish,[31] it ought to be demolished and destroyed so a new and radical future ushered by YHWH can come into existence.

Once these human constructions that have restrained the understanding of God are demolished new things can be born. Oswalt ties this passage with times in history in which God has broken out of the human-made structures in order to bring renewal, as was the case with "Saint Francis, the Pietists, the Reformation, the Wesleyan revival, and most recently, the charismatic movement."[32] One of the foremost examples of times of renewal is found in the life of the Spirit-filled New Testament church. It is during this period that God sends out the Jewish disciples as a missionary people that would stretch as far as the ends of the world, reaching the gentiles. When this happened, Greek thought within the Roman empire was the most immediate encounter the church experienced. In this context the apostle Paul appropriates the words of Isaiah, as he usually does in "sections that are of

---

29. Oswalt, *Book of Isaiah*, 356.
30. Hays, *First Corinthians*, 29.
31. Hebrew אבד (*'ābad*).
32. Oswalt, *Book of Isaiah*, 356.

fundamental importance for his reasoning,"³³ turning to his favorite source he quotes:

> As God says in the Scriptures, "I will destroy the wisdom of all who claim to be wise. I will confuse those who think they know so much." (1 Cor 1:19 CEV)

For Wilk, the remarkable correspondence between 1 Cor 1 and Isa 29 LXX shows that "Paul was well aware of the Old Testament context when quoting Isa. 29.14b. However, whereas the verse in its original context concerns Israel, Paul has applied it to humankind in general."³⁴ The work of Christ at the cross defies both Jewish and Greek expectations. Perhaps both cultures encompass the whole human experience when faced with the divine. Once again human understanding finds itself at odds with the ways of God; therefore, God decides once again to ruin and destroy³⁵ these human constructions of what the divine should do. Of course, from Paul's perspective the cross is actually the fulfillment of Isaiah.³⁶

The theologian Martin Luther followed Paul's steps in rendering foolish the wisdom of the wise when he confronted what he termed "theology of glory," a representation of the theological system of medieval Aristotelianism, against a "theology of the cross." Central to this theology of the cross are the concept and practice of *destructio*, the Latin translation of Paul's ’απολῶ (*apolō*), which according to Crowe sometimes points to the critical work of the "theologian of the cross" and is concerned with the practical application of truth for the human good, for example in salvation.³⁷

Luther was not only a great influence in Heidegger's intellectual development but also in his idea of philosophy as *destruktion*, a Germanized version of the Latin *destructio*. Even when the term is never unequivocally defined by Heidegger himself, the overall

---

33. Wilk, "Isaiah in 1 and 2 Corinthians," 157.
34. Wilk, "Isaiah in 1 and 2 Corinthians," 137.
35. Greek ’απολῶ (*apolō*).
36. Wilk, "Isaiah in 1 and 2 Corinthians," 156.
37. Crowe, *Heidegger's Religious Origins*, 45, 48, 62.

use in his work shows it "is taken to be an activity that is primarily aimed at helping secure the proper *theory* about human life by critically examining traditional ideas."[38] Crowe claims that the ultimate purpose of *destruktion* is positive because it attempts "to *liberate* or *free up* [*überliefern*] possibilities from the past for the sake of the future."[39]

It is Heidegger's *destruktion* that Algerian-French philosopher Jacques Derrida finally translates as *déconstruction*.[40] One could trace a connection of ideas associated with deconstruction across these many figures: from the prophet Isaiah, to the apostle Paul, to the theologian Luther, to the philosopher Heidegger, and lastly to the also philosopher Derrida. Of course, it would be naïve to pretend that such history means all authors meant the same or would even agree with each other's conclusions; their contexts and concerns were very different. But, at the risk of being anachronistic, we could say there is a shared realization among all these authors that calcified ideas can hinder humans from enjoying a renewed future.

But what exactly is deconstruction in the context of faith? It is explained as "the dismantling of anything that's been constructed. . . . Theological deconstruction, as such, is the process of dismantling one's accepted beliefs."[41] Brian Zahnd's description, "a crisis of Christian faith that leads to either a reevaluation of Christianity or sometimes a total abandonment of Christianity,"[42] shows deconstruction can reconfigure the whole of one's life. Kenneth Archer's succinct definition, "the desert of skeptical criticism,"[43] points us to the possibility of intense emotional and intellectual strain. If we take into account the relationship between deconstruction, the prophetic tradition of Isaiah, and the community in Corinth, perhaps we could suggest the Spirit of God has always

38. Crowe, *Heidegger's Religious Origins*, 45, 47, 236.
39. Crowe, *Heidegger's Religious Origins*, 260.
40. Caputo, *Cross and Cosmos*, 71–76.
41. Swoboda, *After Doubt*, 7.
42. Zahnd, *When Everything Is On Fire*, 26.
43. Archer, *Pentecostal Hermeneutic*, 7.

been a force that destroys certain aspects of our faith so these can be born anew. This would mean that the Spirit guides believers into a better understanding of faith and a deeper relationship with God, when hardened beliefs have hindered believers from faithfully following God.

Of course, such assertion is bound to produce pushback. As mentioned in the previous section, deconstruction has been discredited in evangelical circles sometimes with good arguments but many times by ill-informed opinions born from defensive or dismissive postures. Because of this I think it is important to learn from the source, not in order to agree with the theology of people like Derrida or Caputo, but to learn about the deconstructive way of thinking and finding ways it can be addressed in order to pastor and disciple believers.

In 1994 Villanova University held a round table with Jacques Derrida in the midst of launching the university's new doctoral program in philosophy. The conversation was led by John Caputo who later presented this exchange as a book with significant commentaries in which he elaborates Derrida's responses. The result has been celebrated as an influential work regarding the relationship of theology and deconstruction. In this book Derrida gives important explanations that help us understand deconstruction from his perspective.

From this work, titled *Deconstruction in a Nutshell*, I have identified six sayings Jacques Derrida uses to explain what exactly is deconstruction and what it is not: (1) deconstruction happens, (2) deconstruction happens from inside, (3) deconstruction is not a method, (4) deconstruction is a call, (5) deconstruction is a yes to the other, and (6) deconstruction is affirmative of institutions ... is not destruction.[44] Summed up together these sayings serve as helpful guide in explaining what deconstruction really is about; it is also very helpful that this book provides an extended commentary from Caputo, who helpfully sets the subject in the environment of faith.

---

44. Caputo, *Deconstruction in a Nutshell*, 5–27.

Conclusion

As a pastor in Latin America, I find much more influence from deconstructive theology than postliberal theology in the local church context. It is important to remember that both are very critical of modernity, but their approaches and conclusions are very different. Postliberals find great value in the church as a community of believers while deconstructionists tend to be wary about it. Deconstructive theology can also be very lax in its commitment to orthodoxy, Caputo sets an example by being very transparent about his Roman Catholic roots while also dismissing orthodox Catholic beliefs.

Factors like the ones just mentioned have led evangelical circles to discredit deconstruction, but I believe it can be used in the discipleship of believers if we address it correctly. The effects of deconstructive theology are already making an impact in Latin American churches, directly affecting the lives of many believers who, in many cases, receive dismissive or defensive responses from their pastors. Because Pentecostalism represents a major religious movement in Latin American churches at the moment, deconstructive theology in the Latin American context must be addressed from a Christian Pentecostal perspective informed by the pastoral ministry.

In order to highlight its relevance to the Latin American Pentecostal context, I have extended the conversation of each of Derrida's six sayings with three related subsections: the subject's perspective from the Costa Rican religious context which can serve a model for other contextualized approaches, a brief conversation of these sayings in relation to Peter's experience in the house of Cornelius, and finally, an approach from the Pentecostal tradition. Each of these subsections will ultimately lead to addressing deconstruction in the current context of Latin American Pentecostal faith communities in urban areas.

2

Deconstruction Happens

"Deconstruction is something which happens."[1]

—J. Derrida

From Derrida's perspective we are born into a world of *différance*, where multiple and overlapping matrices of meaning are already in place, we are part of them, even when they started without us; because of this, deconstruction is highly suspicious of the idea of an autonomous ego that simply decides to deconstruct. Deconstruction is not something we primarily do; it is better understood as something that happens to us; because, as we well see ahead, deconstruction is not a method we impose to a certain subject but a call we respond to.

This response is precisely where humans have some agency regarding deconstruction. We participate in deconstructive processes either by promoting them via maintaining an open posture or by resisting them and trying to prevent them; the second option is not the best since the unrelenting event will likely take place whether

1. Caputo, *Deconstruction in a Nutshell*, 9.

we like it or not.² For Caputo such a process comes from God (an unorthodox version of God as we will see, but still God). We may not invite God, but he still comes uninvited to shatter our misdirected conceptions: "God, what is going on in the name of God, is not a projection but a projectile headed straight at us, a missile upending our narcissistic desires, a visitation that comes without invitation."³ What is left for us is not defining if we want to deal with deconstructive forces, but how we decide to deal with them.

Costa Rican Context: Unexpected, Unrelenting Forces

Deconstruction is not a philosophical proposition with no consequences in the real world. Events with the power to profoundly transform, or deconstruct, our worldview and faith can happen when we least expect it. This is evident when we look at the history of the encounter between the pre-Columbian Latin American populations and the European colonialists.

Christopher Columbus first arrived in America in the year 1492 while trying to find a direct way from Western Europe to Asia. This was the age of the "Catholic Kings," a time in which "Spain was entering upon the age of its greatest power and the decisive construction of its image as the standard-bearer of Catholicism."⁴ The times of relative tolerance between Christianity, Judaism, and Islam in that area were over. The long crusades shaped the identity of the empire, creating an intolerant and violent atmosphere. The elite's desire for political and religious orthodoxy resulted in the creation of the infamous Inquisition which indicates a significant shift in theological history. In previous times the patristic treatment of heretical ideas focused on the threat heresy represented to the Christian faith; the Inquisition, on the other hand, was more

---

2. See Caputo, *Folly of God*, 26.
3. Caputo, *Hoping against Hope*, 125.
4. Hastings, *World History of Christianity*, 328.

Deconstruction Happens

concerned with protecting individuals and institutions, branding many movements as heretical for political reasons.[5]

The accidental arrival to American lands was interpreted as an act of God that confirmed the special role of Spain in history and the divine support of the Catholic kings. In 1493 Pope Alexander VI granted the kings of Spain and Portugal the *patronato*, "total responsibility for evangelization of all the new lands their subjects were uncovering."[6] This allowed religious and political authorities to justify an invasion as evangelization. This evangelistic campaign was led primarily by conquistadores, a group of men chiefly motivated by the love of gold and making a name for themselves.

It took ten years after the first Spanish incursion in the Americas for the Spaniards to find their way to Costa Rica. In 1502 Columbus himself arrived in the Atlantic coast now known today as Limón. According to calculations made by bishop Thiel, at the time of the Spanish conquest there were 27,000 indigenous people in Costa Rica distributed among five different tribes. Many Costa Ricans at the time believed in *Sibú*, the Supreme Being who gave origin to men and nature by planting seeds; they worshiped natural elements such as the Sun and the Moon. Historian Ricardo Fernández asserts that even when native peoples such as the Chorotegas (located on the opposite side of where Columbus first arrived) were always submissive to the Spaniards, this did not stop the conquerors from treating them in the cruelest ways, almost completely obliterating a smart, cult, and gallant people.[7] This treatment of aboriginal people by the Spaniards was very similar in all of Latin America, leading to the collapse of aboriginal populations throughout the Spanish-conquered territories; this in turn, prompted the "importation of black slaves from Africa to replace the natives they were wiping out."[8]

The violent conquest came hand-in-hand with the first experience of the gospel for Latin Americans. In 1522, for example,

5. McGrath, *Heresy*, 208.
6. Hastings, *World History of Christianity*, 329.
7. Fernández Guardia, *Historia de Costa Rica*, 9.
8. Hastings, *World History of Christianity*, 332.

Deconstruction and the Spirit

the Catholic leader Diego de Agüero claimed to have baptized and converted six thousand Chorotega people in Costa Rica, even when neither group understood each other's language at the time.[9] From that moment on Costa Rica defined its religious identity as distinctly Catholic, to the point that even now the country remains as one of the few officially confessional states in the world.

The encounter between Spaniards and Costa Ricans *just happened* from the Costa Rican indigenous perspective, they knew nothing about the results of a trip made by accident by these sailors a decade before. The unexpected meeting completely transformed the worldview and day-to-day reality of entire people groups. This produced an ever-growing complexity of the Costa Rican experience in all arenas of life. Regarding religion, aboriginal spirituality was overcome by Catholic faith which in time would be forced to also endure other expressions of faith.

By 1840s the first Protestant service in Costa Rica was celebrated by North American, British, and German citizens, surrounded by a religiously intolerant atmosphere. The railroad construction by Afro-Caribbeans provided the opportunity for the first Protestant missions in the country; these where first carried out by the Jamaican Baptists Missionary Society in 1887. Other protestant missionary endeavors followed afterwards: Wesleyan Methodists in 1894, Anglicans in 1896, Seventh Day Adventists in 1903, and Salvation Army 1907. Pentecostal missionaries started arriving around ten years after the Azusa Street's Revival in 1918.[10]

No Protestants died in Costa Rica because of religious intolerance as did happen in other Central American countries. Nevertheless, non-Catholic believers were victims of violence on a regular basis, not just by being publicly humiliated, but it was common that stones would be thrown at them, their houses, and churches. Many even experienced discrimination and negligence when receiving medical attention, to the point that an evangelical

---

9. Holland, *Religión en Costa Rica*, 1.
10. Holland, *Religión en Costa Rica*, 2.

Deconstruction Happens

hospital, Clínica Bíblica, had to be opened in 1929 to guarantee the correct medical attention of non-Catholic patients.[11]

Between 1946 and 1982 the evangelical movement in Costa Rica started developing at a fast rate. Different evangelical ministries with nationwide impact started flourishing such as radio stations, schools, camps, missionary institutions, pastoral schools, and countrywide evangelistic campaigns. By 1978 the twelve biggest Protestant denominations in the country summed up 513 local churches holding together 32,038 people.[12]

All the upheaval that resulted in the present Latin American reality came to be by the accidental encounter of two peoples who were not even looking for each other. Human greed and perversion distorted what could have been a reciprocally benefiting experience. Derrida's simple assertion, the recognition that it just "happens," points us to the human experience of the unexpected. This brief historical account shows humans are constantly and unexpectedly exposed to forces strong enough to reshape our understanding of the world, impact our beliefs, and literally change the trajectory of our lives.

The belief systems of whole nations changed by an unexpected encounter. This is the sad history of the gift of the gospel in Latin America. Once the encounter happened it could not be undone. There is no use in blaming the casual bystanders at the beach. Once they saw the weird looking strangers in the boat, they could not unsee them. Something is bound to happen with the potential of bringing great gifts or great pain, many times both. Such is the nature of deconstructive experiences: they happen. The question is *how* can we approach them.

---

11. Holland, *Historia de la Iglesia Evangélica*, 17–18.
12. Holland, *Historia de la Iglesia Evangélica*, 19, 21.

Peter in the House of Cornelius: Deconstruction Happens

Once upon a time, there was an apostle to whom something just happened, something that would change his faith life forever as well as history itself. The book of Acts chapter 10 narrates the encounter between the apostle Peter and Cornelius, a man that could be described as a successful leader, a disciplined person, a family man, or a devout believer; but in Peter's eyes he was primarily a gentile. The apostle was about to have an experience that would dismantle his mental constructions about Cornelius and the other gentiles, and ultimately his conception about what God could and would do. This event would cause a personal crisis in him that would lead him to reevaluate how he practiced his faith, but first he would skeptically critique the whole experience. Perhaps we could say Peter was about to have his faith deconstructed.

The spiritual experience both men had would sound very familiar to any Latin American Pentecostal. Both positioned themselves to be exposed to God's voice by faithfully searching for him. Cornelius had a revelatory experience, a vision that provided instructions;[13] Peter underwent an ecstatic trance[14] that would defy core beliefs. This was a divine initiative they could not elicit. They could only position themselves to be exposed to what the Spirit of God was preparing. From their perspective *it just happened*. God was about to do something new and the faithful apostle, a direct disciple of the incarnated Christ, filled with the Spirit, was about to be further transformed.

The Bible points us to the reality that unexpected circumstances can profoundly transform human beings. It is easier to see the agency of God when we have a biblical author making explicit connections; it may be harder to discern it in more recent historical events. But we cannot deny that from a biblical perspective the Spirit actively moves so his people can be transformed.

---

13. Greek, ὁράματι (*horamati*).
14. Greek, ἔκστασις (*ekstasis*).

Pentecostal Perspective: The Spirit is Actively Making Things Happen

The Pentecostal movement feels at home when it comes to unexpected happenings. Even when Pentecostalism is not denominational per se but a "renewal movement that emphasizes the experience of God,"[15] one can identify distinctive Christian beliefs among those who partake in the Pentecostal identity. One of the movement's core tenets identified by Albrecht and Howard is the belief in Christ the Spirit-Baptizer and Sanctifier. This belief finds expression in the Pentecostal understanding of the Spirit as constantly active: "Pentecostals expect the Holy Spirit to speak to them, to touch their hearts through strong emotions, to reveal something of God to them through ideas and pictures that come to their minds or through dreams."[16]

Pentecostals expect the unexpected in the Spirit,[17] even if the experience itself is not necessarily as supernatural as a vision or a trance; the main idea is that the Spirit is always at work in surprising ways. This pneumatological imagination[18] drives Pentecostal Christianity to a "radical openness to God . . . a fundamental openness to alterity or otherness . . . to the continuing (and sometimes surprising) operations of the Spirit in church

---

15. Albrecht and Howard, "Pentecostal Spirituality," 235.

16. Albrecht and Howard, "Pentecostal Spirituality," 237.

17. Wariboko and Yong point out that Pentecostals and Evangelicals agree in seeing the Spirit as one who bridges Scripture to the present time, "but in its more radical forms, Pentecostals insist that the revelatory work of the Spirit manifest in and through the apostolic experience remains ongoing today, and in that sense there is the possibility of new truths that the Spirit will unfold through new experiences and in different times and places (even if some might then draw back in saying such new truth will neither contradict nor be inconsistent with what the Bible says)." Even when this radical belief would be marginal in the Costa Rican context, the driving force behind it would be true for Costa Rican Pentecostals even when most would identify with the belief in a Spirit who never contradicts the Bible. See Wariboko and Yong, *Paul Tillich and Pentecostal Theology*, 8.

18. Wariboko and Yong, *Paul Tillich and Pentecostal Theology*, 8.

and world."[19] This conception of the world gives Pentecostalism a distinctively playful character[20] with a tremendous capacity for adaptation and resilience.

Being informed by Hannah Arendt's political philosophy, Nimi Wariboko affirms, "The event of Pentecost is an affirmation of the miraculous nature of human action, that capacity to begin something new, the articulation of *natality*."[21] He talks about five natalities: (1) spiritual natality, a conversion experience; (2) factual natality, a daily crucifixion and renewal; (3) political natality, moving beyond the beginning of someone to the beginning of something by the gifts and empowerment of the Spirit; (4) *philos*-natality, a birth to friendship with God and others even to the point of erasing color and class divides as seen in the Azusa Street revival and Pentecost itself; and (5) temporal natality, a break with the world's automatism into a renewed sense of reality and new rhythms of existence. These natalities illustrate the multiform impact of Christ in the life of the believer through the Spirit, constantly remaking and renewing oneself according to God's will.

When the Pentecostal imagination runs into unforeseen events, it assumes a listening posture to the move of the Holy Spirit with a playful and sensitive heart. Pentecostals wholeheartedly believe God is constantly making things happen.

---

19. Smith, *Thinking in Tongues*, 12.

20. According to Suurmond it is precisely this playful character that differentiates Pentecostal liturgy from mainline and Catholic church services. See Suurmond, *Word and Spirit at Play*, 220.

21. Wariboko, *Pentecostal Principle*, 20. See also his section on "Natality and Pentecostalism," 134–41.

3

Deconstruction Happens from Inside

"Deconstruction is something which happens and which happens from inside."[1]

—J. Derrida

DECONSTRUCTION HAPPENS FROM WITHIN; this can be seen in two senses. First, as we will see later, there is already a deconstructive element present within ideas. For example, dominating binaries (like male or white) *define themselves* by what *they are not* (female or black). Watkin explains, "Deconstruction, then, is what happens: things deconstruct or, better, things exist deconstructively."[2] Consequently, it is said that deconstruction happens in the middle voice; things deconstruct. For this reason, Derrida asserts deconstruction is not neutral; it directly intervenes because it is already inside.[3]

1. Caputo, *Deconstruction in a Nutshell*, 9.
2. Watkin, *Jacques Derrida*, 23.
3. See Derrida, *Positions*, 93.

Deconstruction and the Spirit

This leads to the second sense in which it can be said that deconstruction happens from inside. The modern ideal pretends to analyze things from the outside by using external methodologies, but deconstruction does not happen from an objective vantage point, unpolluted by the object of study. Deconstruction celebrates subjectivity, the complete immersion within the world we try to understand. It is important to clarify that the understanding of subjectivity in postmodern thought does not allow for the modernist conceptions of radical individualism. It is not up to the individual to simply decide what is true because she is irremediably immersed within the intricate matrices of meaning. Downing clarifies this position: "Humans are not autonomous subjects entirely in control of their perception. . . . Subjectivity for the postmodernist, then, is not individualistic; it is corporate, reflecting a community's model of truth. . . . Our subjectivity operates in response to objective truths, but our knowledge of those truths is always implicated by the models that shape our subject positions."[4]

Costa Rican Context: Memory

Postmodern thought reminds us of the importance of location. We are forever immersed in particular contexts that shape how we experience the world and understand the meaning of things. We are deeply shaped by our history and memories.

"You are your memories," said Nobel Prize winner Eric Kandel when interviewed by cofounder of Omaze Ryan Cummins.[5] Kandel's groundbreaking studies of memory are motivated by his earliest, most painful memories: fleeing Vienna, Austria, as a child, in order to escape the Nazi invasion. Kandel found that our regular experiences are assigned to short-term memories where they are quickly forgotten, yet those highly sensitized experiences (e.g., painful or highly rewarding) go to our brain's long-term

---

4. Downing, *How Postmodernism Serves (My) Faith*, 139–40.
5. Cummings, "You Are Your Memories."

Deconstruction Happens from Inside

memories. These memories and what we learn from them end up defining who we are.

For Fritz Kling, painful memories can also be experienced on a collective level; according to him, "Postcolonialism is the world's most common form of memory."[6] Colonialism works in the symbolic world of oppressed peoples by forcing the empire's symbols to the cultural center as the norm, the moral, the rational; while the colonies' belief systems are relegated to the periphery and regarded as weak, inferior, and superstitious.

Europe itself was once at the margin. When Enrique Dussel addresses the two hegemonic inversions whose effects have distorted the history of Christianity, the first one he identifies is the reversal of a marginal messianic community of Christians to the imperial religion; the second inversion is the geopolitical shift caused by Europe's coming to America. This caused a shift from an interregional system that used to gravitate around "west of China ... Hindustan and the Islamic world" to a "world system" in which the once peripheral Western Europe now occupied the center. Now, the newly appointed center of the world rejected the "peripheric" American cultures as inferior.[7]

The impossibility of differentiating between the violence of colonization from the violence of evangelization is exemplified by the use Christian baptism was given in some instances according to historian Moacir de Castro Maia, who says Christian baptism was instrumentalized in the making of a new slave. When Africans were forcefully brought to America this sacrament would be used as symbol of thorough desocialization.[8] No wonder why colonialism is called "the dark side of modernity."[9] There is no denying Christianity was manipulated as an instrument of oppression in many instances; yet, a great number of Latin Americans have assumed the Christian faith and made it a core part of their identity.

---

6. Kling, *Meeting of the Waters*, 177.
7. Dussel, "Epistemological Decolonization of Theology," 23.
8. Barreto, "Decoloniality and Interculturality," 77–78.
9. Tamez, "Lectura Latinoamericana y Caribeña," 170.

Deconstruction and the Spirit

But, again, we must be aware of our memories. Kling continues to say, "The ingrained cultural norms that persist after colonial rule can include servility, complacency, distrust, resentment, and most of all, dependency. . . . Memory, by definition, lingers."[10] While sentiments of distrust and resentment of Latin Americans towards the Vatican or Evangelical Christianity from the United States are probably more present among the non-believers, other attitudes such as servility, complacency, and dependency towards Evangelical Christianity from the United States can definitely be found among Latin American Pentecostals. From Londoño's perspective Christianity in Latin America "ends up benefiting the white, the European or North American, and their missionary armies";[11] even if this may be the case in *some* circumstances one should always be wary to use blanket statements, there are plenty of examples of selfless missionary work done by North American and European brothers and sisters throughout Latin American history. It is my perception that the biggest challenge right now is how many Latin American believers mirror theologies and practices that have a strong North American taste, uncritically assuming that these churches from the North know better. Even though Costa Rica has been independent since 1821, some colonial attitudes seem to persist, which is why many prefer to see postcolonialism more as *de-colonialism*, an ongoing process of reaffirming a people's identity.

Postcolonial readings of the Bible acknowledge that the idea of an impartial and objective author or reader is merely a construction.[12] Postcolonialism does not wait passively for intercultural exchanges to transform realities but unapologetically deconstructs any ideas of cultural superiority that have distorted history. Postcolonialism affirms the polycentric reality of world Christianity; it makes room "for creative reconstructions and reinventions of,

---

10. Kling, *Meeting of the Waters*, 177–78.
11. Londoño, "Hermenéuticas Postcoloniales," 3–4.
12. Tamez, "Lectura Latinoamericana y Caribeña," 171.

among other things, Latin American religious identities,"[13] and allows the possibility of a more authentic mutual learning.

Empowerment is key for critically addressing foreign ideas. Escobar highlights the usefulness of *contextualization* in the face of the Latin American reality: "[Contextualization] may also be understood in a more general way as a movement that seeks to affirm local cultures in their search for autonomy and full expression, as a reactive process in contrast to globalization. . . . Bible translation in the vernacular has been a decisive factor in the strengthening of a sense of identity and dignity of peoples and nations, thus preparing them to struggle against colonialism."[14] In the same way that Bible translation was a key factor in helping Latin Americans appropriate their faith by allowing them to own and reshape what once was a mere imposition, I think theological education can further the process of empowerment that started with access to the biblical texts by leveling the power differentials between local faith communities and foreign voices.

Yet, theological education is not the forte of the Costa Rican Pentecostal church—this is probably true in most of Latin America. Misconceptions about education as a hindrance to the direction of the Holy Spirit have led many leaders to favor secular theological education (which obviously helps to some point) over nonsecular theological education. The Costa Rican Pentecostal movement that started a bold expansion in the seventies and eighties recruited young people who would devote their lives to ministry with an eschatological urge to evangelize before the imminent return of Christ. This urgent need for evangelization led to tremendous numerical growth but left no place for furthering the minimum theological preparation many of these leaders received. It is understandable that past generations of Costa Rican Pentecostal leaders lacked the theological tools necessary for a robust theological exchange, consequently *importing* tendencies more than *producing* them.

---

13. Barreto, "Decoloniality and Interculturality," 83.
14. Escobar, *New Global Mission*, 61–62.

Deconstruction and the Spirit

To some degree these dynamics are being repeated in the present regarding the issue of deconstruction of faith. Costa Rican believers and leaders in a globalized world receive the influence of deconstructing movements from the global West and end up either uncritically mirroring them or blindly rejecting them. In my opinion, critical engagement should be our approach, but the empowerment of education is necessary for this to happen.

Latin American theologian Justo González provides a good picture of what critical engagement should look like. González sees the expansion of the church in Acts as a series of conversions using the paradigm of frontiers versus borders. Frontiers are unidirectional and impermeable, the result of mythologies such as Manifest Destiny that assume a conquering posture. Borders, on the other hand, are bidirectional places of encounter; their permeability allows for mutual transformation and growth. True borders lead to *mestizaje*,[15] a truly intimate encounter. For González, the church in Acts expands by setting borders, constantly learning from new contexts, leading to different conversions of the church along the way. The mission of the church is expanded by *mestizaje*.[16] This is the kind of mutual exchange that needs to happen in the immediate future of Christianity between Latin American and Western theologies, as well as between Latin American theologies and theologies from the rest of the Majority World; a mutual exchange that allows a natural movement from philosophical conversations to lived ecclesiologies.

Memories help us understand ourselves, allowing us to better relate to others and to find new ways into the future. The Costa Rican Pentecostal Christian church should understand itself as being located within a context of well-educated and world-connected people who possess a strong democratic mindset[17] that allows for

---

15. A term that started being used in a pejorative sense to describe the offspring born of Spanish and native relationships.

16. González, *Santa Biblia*, 86–87.

17. Costa Rica is recognized as one of the strongest democracies in Latin America. This profound democratic tradition shapes the Costa Rican understanding of and relationship to authority.

the possibility of robust dialogue. Its Pentecostalism is full of vitality; it carries the seeds of the promise of being raised by the Spirit as dreamers and prophets. Its Christianity connects the church's identity to a long history of disciples and traditions that have much to teach a church in the midst of a postmodern reality.

Peter in the House of Cornelius: The Inside of What Happens

The only way Peter can relate in a new way to the gentiles is from his location as a Jew. He is not able to objectively analyze the situation, so God finds him amid his core identity through an experience in the middle voice (ἐγένετο ἐπ' αὐτὸν ἔκστασις Acts 10:10), precisely the way deconstruction is supposed to *happen*. By showing Peter the unexpected, God was revealing the matrices of meaning the apostle was dealing with; a seed was being planted that would not bear fruit until later.

God insists three times (as he usually dealt with the apostle) while Peter clung tight to the dietary laws. William Willimon grasps the significance of these matrices of meaning from the minority's point of view: "[they are] people for whom a bit of pork or a pinch of incense or a little intermarriage was a matter of life and death for the community . . . a matter of survival and identity for Jews . . . can it be that these laws are being supplanted by some other basis for survival and identity?"[18] This insight is very significant: laws, structures, and traditions can have more weight to minorities because these represent a safeguard for an endangered identity. The danger for Christians is when faith communities place more importance on methods and customs than they do on their identity as disciples of Christ. This distinction is many times invisible, until the Spirit invites us into experiences that reframe our hearts. Peter's memory probably triggered sentiments of distrust and resentment towards gentiles; after all, the impure beasts shown to him represented how he perceived gentiles. The great

---

18. Willimon, *Acts*, 95.

miracle in this story is that those at the center and those at the margins find a place of mutual learning and growth.

The lingering effect of memory as mentioned by Kling and the patience God showed in dealing with the apostle three times show us to be sensitive to other people's beliefs and traditions, even if these need to be challenged. Important change takes times but also requires a steady effort. Like in the case of Peter, God finds us where we are to take us where he wants us to be. Our faith in the incarnated Christ reminds us God finds no problem with the gift of subjectivity. He walks with us in the midst of our human experience.

Pentecostal Perspective: The Embodied Experience of the Spirit

Downing addresses the subjectivity of human experience and the multiple matrices of meaning by calling them "constructive towers of knowledge."[19] She proceeds to describe a tower encircled by a bigger tower which in turn is encircled by a third even bigger tower and so on. We do not come to these towers; we are born into them. The first tower is our family, the second would be our gender, race, and ethnicity, the third our social class, then our neighborhood and country and finally, our historical era. The different values that guide our interaction with the world are written in the walls of these towers (e.g., "share your toys"; "men do this, not that"; "these kind of people are not trustworthy"; "God expects. . .") and

---

19. Downing, *How Postmodernism Serves (My) Faith*, 155–78. The author clarifies she did not specify a tower of religion because religion functions in different ways depending on each person; for some people religious affiliation is a matter of class while for others it is a matter of ethnicity. Yet, she does recognize the important role of religion within the towers of knowledge. From a Catholic perspective, for example, Protestants raised the tower of the infallibility of the Bible in exchange for the belief in a Spirit-inspired Pope. When this concept is combined with the belief in the "priesthood of all believers" a multiplicity of biblical interpretations arise that contribute to postmodern relativism and the further division of the church (the multiple towers of Lutherans, Episcopalians, Pentecostals, and many others).

no matter how hard we try we are always surrounded by different towers. The multiple towers around us determine in many ways our responsiveness to God, but also point us to the sovereignty of a God who placed us there when we were born.

Downing continues to explain we may not fully escape the influence of these towers, but through *agency* we can rewrite in important ways the discourse of said towers. This is especially important for people on the margins who many times live in the intersection of two or more towers, which is Downing's description of the postcolonial experience. She also makes the important remark that God not only places us within determined human-made towers that define our experience but he also transcends said towers. In consequence, transcending human-made towers would make God unconditioned by these constructions. God can find us where we are and helps us change what needs to be rewritten. From this perspective, the location of a person within her or his towers of meaning is something to be honored as part of God's sovereignty, even if it sometimes requires to be challenged, as any human construction needs to be; this also means humans can be empowered by God to rewrite unjust, sinful, or erred messages within their surrounding towers. Pentecostalism is well equipped to deal with the reality from this viewpoint in at least three ways.

First, Pentecostalism is an embodied experience that finds a person's location as something that should be both honored and challenged. It traces its identity back to the events described in Acts 2, which represent a highly subjective but deeply communal experience. Tongues of fire rested on them enabling each one to speak as the Spirit willed, but far from isolating them in individualistic mystical experiences, the Spirit united them as a community of faith, assigning each one an important role in the body of believers by enabling them to communicate in different languages through *xenolalia*.[20] Such enabling not only brought the community of disciples together, but it also connected them to the

---

20. Even glossolalia in the community of faith is meant to connect us to others through interpretation, as seen in 1 Corinthians.

multiple experiences of those from other towers of knowledge: Parthians, Medes, Phrygians, and many others.

The Pentecost experience honors the location of each individual while also challenging them to rewrite the walls of their towers through a call to faith and repentance, while bonding them into a community of faith. Tillich identifies that "in the story of Pentecost, the Spirit of Christ shows its creativity in both directions, the individual and the universal."[21] Wariboko resonates with this posture: "Pentecostalism renders all distinctions, divisional markings, and classes inoperative without abolishing them and 'without ever reaching any final ground,' engendering a tension within every identity itself."[22]

The ultimate sign of a person's location is one's own body, that which allows us to inhabit space and time, placing us firmly within different towers of meaning. Pentecostalism unapologetically affirms embodiment and materiality. The Pentecostal value of the supernatural finds very material manifestations. Pentecostal preaching itself is the preamble to embodied experiences in the Spirit such as prayer for divine healing; "deliverance and liberation, then, are not just 'spiritual.' . . . Implicit in this affirmation of bodily healing is a broader affirmation, namely, a sense that the full gospel values the *whole* person."[23] Smith even expands to explain the affinity Pentecostalism has found with the so called prosperity gospel: "The prosperity gospel (for all its failures) might be an unwitting testimony to the holism of Pentecostal spirituality. . . . [Such testimony is] one of the most un-Gnostic moments of Pentecostal spirituality that refuses to spiritualize the promise that the gospel is 'good news for the poor.'"[24] Without a doubt this is

---

21. Tillich, *Shaking of the Foundations*, 138.

22. Wariboko, *Pentecostal Principle*, 143.

23. Smith, *Thinking in Tongues*, 42. Smith rightly recognizes the fact that Pentecostalism has uncritically adopted fundamentalist dualisms, yet, as shown, said dualisms do not harmonize with the Pentecostal worldview. This, in my opinion, is one of the lingering effects of a colonial memory in Latin American Pentecostalism that simply imports ideas without critical engagement out of a sense of inferiority.

24. Smith, *Thinking in Tongues*, 43.

one of the reasons Pentecostalism (with a clear bent towards prosperity) has found open arms in believing communities throughout Latin America.

Second, Pentecostalism empowers those on the margins. Pentecostals boldly appropriate Christ's promise "but you shall receive power when the Holy Spirit comes upon you" (Acts 1:8), a verse as famous as John 3:16 within Latin American Pentecostal communities. Albrecht and Howard explain, "Immediately prior to the Pentecostal revivals, Christians were eagerly seeking the power of God: power for abundant living, power for victory over sin, power for effective witness to the world. In the experience of the baptism in the Spirit, Pentecostals found that power."[25] Even if there is no access to medical attention, there is access to the healing power of God; even if there is an imminent physical threat, there is power over every force that seeks to harm, oppress, or destroy; even if there is human suffering, there is power to flourish and prosper, all through the Spirit's empowerment.

Third, the Pentecostal experience values and even expects emotional responses. This is an important postmodern posture because modernity disdained the highly subjective aspect of emotional reactions while favoring supposedly objective rational responses. The modern myth that was supposed to lead humans to better engagement with the surrounding world backfired by disconnecting us from realities; as Smith notes, "emotions are not just reflexive responses or the 'irrational' detritus of experience. Emotions are themselves 'takes' on the world."[26] Furthermore, Joel B. Green states, "Brain lesion studies have demonstrated that damage to the emotion-processing center of the brain impedes real-life rationality and decision-making."[27] We could say that in order to be rational, one needs to be emotional.

This is especially valuable in a context that suppresses the expression of emotions like Latin American chauvinist societies, where the display of certain emotions is rendered incompatible

---

25. Albrecht and Howard, "Pentecostal Spirituality," 243.
26. Smith, *Thinking in Tongues*, 78.
27. Green, *Body, Soul, and Human Life*, 121.

with the male-female binary (more on binaries in the next section) and is only acceptable if the male is intoxicated with alcohol. Pentecostalism deconstructs this binary by providing a context in which men sing, shout, dance, and cry in the presence of God, something which is celebrated by the whole community.

All these factors bring the community together as part of the story of God's continual action through the presence of the Spirit, providing individuals not only a sense of agency, but shared purpose; "[offering a] narratival location—situating the believing community within a story that provides a new context for understanding their experience."[28] This is salvation as embodied transformation.[29]

On a global scale, a Latin American Pentecostalism that furthers its agency through an empowering theological education that provides the tools for critical theological analysis, instead of simple repetition of denominational dogmas or apologetic formulas, will be uniquely positioned to contribute to a grand theological conversation; especially if it rediscovers its Christian roots which transcend Azusa and reach all the way back to Catholic orthodoxy.

On the local scale, Latin American Pentecostalism is more than capable in engaging subjective deconstructive experiences because of the way it embraces and celebrates the subjectivity of the human being in all its uniqueness while firmly planting the human experience within a community of meaning that points to the objective realities of God.

---

28. Smith, *Thinking in Tongues*, 69.
29. See Green, *Body, Soul, and Human Life*, 137–39.

4

Deconstruction Is Not a Method

"Deconstruction is not a method or some tool that you apply something from the outside."[1]

—J. Derrida

EVEN WHEN IT IS tempting to try to reduce deconstruction to a set of steps or methodologies, deconstruction philosophers are very insistent in asserting that deconstruction is not a method. Methods are applied by modern thinkers who use the same set of tools to any given object, under the illusion of being independent and objective observers of phenomena; postmodernism does not claim objectivity and is suspicious of recipe-like approaches that apply the same set of steps independently of what they are analyzing. Watkin explains, "Deconstruction is not a method or a set of procedures that one can pull off the shelf and set to work on any unsuspecting text. . . . A method brings the same set of tools to

1. Caputo, *Deconstruction in a Nutshell*, 9.

everything it encounters . . . it exploits the text for its own purposes, rather than trying to understand the text in its own terms."[2] To say there is such a thing like a deconstructive reading of a text is to treat deconstruction dangerously close to a method. This can be seen in how Derrida tried to be sensible to each specific text by using different terms for what he was doing. Watkin enumerates some of Derrida's terms: deconstruction, *différance*, supplementarity, dissemination, trace, pharmakon, hymen, and iterability.

Perhaps it is Caputo who provides the clearest answer of what exactly is deconstruction by accurately describing it as *a style of thinking*.[3] This means deconstruction is more of an attitude by which we relate to a text, trying to find how authors think. This style of thinking is decidedly inclined towards finding "the tensions, the contradictions, the heterogeneity within [the authors'] own corpus";[4] and is interested in decentering as a way of opening up to the other. Caputo summarizes the deconstructive attitude by stating, "Whenever it runs up against a limit, deconstruction presses against it. . . . Deconstruction is the relentless pursuit of the impossible."[5]

What exactly are these limits deconstruction presses against? Some of the great limits in Western culture are imposed by the "tyranny of binaries," which is a way in which Western metaphysics has structured knowledge while trying to differentiate and explain concepts. For example: big/small, soul/body, male/female, white/black, reason/belief, natural/artificial, heterosexual/homosexual (or any other form of sexuality other than heterosexual), objective/subjective. Even when Derrida recognizes these oppositions might be helpful, he finds two problems with binaries:[6]

---

2. Watkin, *Jacques Derrida*, 21.
3. Caputo, *Folly of God*, 21.
4. Caputo, *Deconstruction in a Nutshell*, 9.
5. Caputo, *Deconstruction in a Nutshell*, 32.
6. See Watkin, *Jacques Derrida*, 12–13.

Hierarchies

Concepts are not just differentiated, they are hierarchized. This leads to the exploitation and oppression of the lesser term. As Downing explains, "in the history of Western culture, most of the top terms were perceived as central to being fully human."[7] Think, for example, about the hierarchized binary male/female; women have suffered from different forms of oppression because they have been assigned the lower status in the binary. Then, the term on top is always preferable; it is easier for a girl to "act as a boy" than for a boy to "act as a girl." Society in fact instrumentalizes language in order to perpetuate this dynamic.

It is important to understand that Derrida never intends to simply reverse hierarchies. This revenge strategy would only perpetuate a flawed system by rearranging the factors without altering the result. Deconstruction is after the hierarchical structure itself, calling it into question because such a structure has been constructed somehow. According to Derrida, these structures of meaning are formed by "forces that are linguistic, historical, social, political, gendered, bodily. . . . Together these forces make up so many matrices—which in the shorthand notation proposed by Derrida is famously called *différance*—which produce relatively stable effects or unities of meaning."[8] Being relatively stable means these units of meaning are also relatively unstable and thus deconstructible. The meaning we assign something is just a freeze frame in time, showing how the forces in the matrices interact at a certain point in history.

Traces

The Western notion of binaries relies on a concept of ideal purity as if one term could exist without the other, while in reality the privileged term is defined in relation to the underprivileged one; e.g., male is that which is not female. Therefore "the dominant

---

7. Downing, *How Postmodernism Serves (My) Faith*, 130.
8. Caputo, *Folly of God*, 24.

term on top gets its meaning by the lower term it rejects. Thus the top term contains a 'trace' of what is not itself."[9] This means the deconstruction of one term is always present from within (deconstruction happens inside). Deconstruction is just exposing that which is already there, creating new ways by destabilizing the categorical oppositions without simply getting rid of binaries.[10] This means deconstruction deals with tensions; it is located in the distance between two opposing ideas. Such distance is conceived as the infinite amount of numbers between zero and one where there is a limitless play of traces; this is called *différance*.[11]

These traces are not restricted to language. The contribution of deconstruction as a style of thinking is to be applied to all areas of human endeavor because one is always located "within a play of differences,"[12] in the midst of *différance*. So, wherever deconstruction finds a dominating binary term, it seeks to remove it from the top of the hierarchy, from the center it has been given; deconstruction is a decentering force that finds new ways.

But then, does deconstruction reject all methodologies and leave us with no tools to engage the world around us? Westphal clarifies that both Derrida and Ricoeur would agree in the importance of methods. Such tools offer necessary guardrails against "anything goes" attitudes,[13] which means that not every perspective or opinion is valid. The problem deconstruction addresses is the modernist blind faith placed in methodologies as deliverers of godlike objectivity.

---

9. Downing, *How Postmodernism Serves (My) Faith*, 131.
10. Watkin, *Jacques Derrida*, 43.
11. See Caputo, *Deconstruction in a Nutshell*, 105, 183–84.
12. Caputo, *Deconstruction in a Nutshell*, 104.
13. Westphal, *Whose Community? Which Interpretation?*, 68.

Costa Rican Context: The Methods of Fundamentalism

As the Protestant movement developed in Costa Rica and Cold War tensions grew worldwide, big ministries from the United States invested heavily in the Central American region. Hastings claims that ministries such as those of Jimmy Swaggart and Pat Robertson proclaimed "a highly anti-Communist and anti-Catholic Gospel of biblical fundamentalism and prosperity"[14] in places like Guatemala. These ministries were also present in Costa Rica during the eighties.

The anti-Communist factor meant a close alignment to Christianity as understood in the United States by fundamentalist right-wing Christians, while the anti-Catholicism of these ministries fanned the flames of a painful history of religious intolerance in Costa Rica, leading to evangelical movements defining themselves further against Catholicism.

Hastings also notes the influence of biblical Fundamentalism. This emerged from the liberal-conservative controversy that took place within North American Protestant Evangelicalism in the first decades of 1900s when a significant group of religious leaders was deeply concerned with the effect modernity exerted over the Christian faith. For history professor Matthew Avery Sutton, Fundamentalists ironically used as much modernist thought and practice as the liberals; in a New York Times piece he describes how "they treated it [the Bible] like an engineering manual. They saw individual verses as pieces of data. . . . Unlike actual religious conservatives, they had no sense of tradition or community. . . . Fundamentalists were highly individualistic and eager to use the latest technology. . . . They had no time for incremental change, or for reasoning with those who differed with them. . . . Jesus was coming soon."[15] Fundamentalists enunciated the irreducible minimum beliefs a person must have in order to be a considered a Christian: "Verbal inspiration and absolute inerrancy of the Scripture, the

---

14. Hastings, *A World History of Christianity*, 365.
15. Sutton, "Day Christian Fundamentalism Was Born," paras. 19, 21.

virgin birth, blood atonement, the bodily resurrection of Christ, the miracle-working power of Christ and the open rejection of the historical-critical method in biblical exegesis."[16] Fundamentalism laid little emphasis on Christian praxis while focusing on "cognitive adherence to 'correct faith' formulation";[17] this produced a sectarian mindset.

Witherup addresses Fundamentalism from the perspective of Catholic biblical interpretation; he defines it as "a loose Protestant movement opposed to modernity and committed to preserving the 'literal' truth of the Bible."[18] However, he identifies positions in the Catholic Church that were essentially fundamentalist prior to the twentieth century (e.g., Pope Leo XIII's *Providentissimus Deus*, which can be seen as a defense of verbal inerrancy). Fundamentalism persists in some Catholic circles because of its appeal as a form of preserving basic biblical values, even when "it is the only approach to biblical interpretation that is singled out officially as incompatible with a Catholic approach."[19] The 1993 Pontifical Biblical Commission states:

> The fundamentalist approach is dangerous, for it is attractive to people who look to the Bible for ready answers to the problems of life. It can deceive this people, offering them interpretations that are pious but illusory. . . . Fundamentalism actually invites people to a kind of intellectual suicide. . . . It unwittingly confuses the divine substance of the biblical message with what are in fact its human limitations.[20]

Gorman classifies Protestantism in three broad groups: Fundamentalist, Evangelicals, and mainline. In order to facilitate analysis, I summarized his insights in the following table.

---

16. Yoder, "Fundamentalism and the Church," 45.
17. Yoder, "Fundamentalism and the Church," 46.
18. Witherup, "Interpretation of the Bible," 202.
19. Witherup, "Interpretation of the Bible," 203.
20. Pontifical Biblical Commission, "Interpretation of the Bible," §I.F.

Branch	Biblical interpretation	Theological, social, and political agendas	Cooperation with other movements
Mainline	General acceptance of biblical criticism	Moderate to liberal	Ecumenical dialogue and cooperation with ideologically similar churches, as well as Roman Catholicism and Orthodoxy.
Evangelical	Gradual and cautious acceptance of biblical criticism	Moderate to conservative	Interdenominational cooperation with ideologically similar traditions. Recently with traditionally Roman Catholics and Orthodox.
Fundamentalist	General rejection of biblical criticism and adherence to theory of Bible's verbal inerrancy	Very conservative in reaction to modernity and perceived liberalism from other churches (often deemed non-churches)	Separatists. Cooperation requires agreements with "fundamentals."

Table 1: Branches of Protestantism by Gorman.[21]

Classifications such as these can be very useful for the sake of clarity but, as it usually happens, we run the risk of oversimplifying complex issues, which is why Gorman clarifies there is a significant overlap among these branches. Most of the Costa Rican Protestant churches move somewhere between Evangelicalism and Fundamentalism, to the point that it is common to hear some critics (and religious leaders) use both terms effectively as synonyms. The overlay of the different tendencies intensifies or diminishes

---

21. Gorman, "Interpretation of the Bible," 178.

depending on the political and social climate or the influence certain ministries exert on different moments and places.

The last element in Hasting's analysis is "prosperity," an ideal that resonated deeply within the Latin American experience. This message was characterized by an overemphasis on the blessing of God over those who faithfully give, and produced leaders whose success was measured by market-like results and strategies.[22]

In 1986 the Assemblies of God developed a project sponsored by Jimmy Swaggart Ministries in which an urban church would be planted in the heart of San José, Costa Rica, by a young Costa Rican pastoral couple; this gave birth to Iglesia Centro Evangelístico in Zapote, the church in which I grew up as the pastor's kid, and in which my wife and I now serve as pastors. Centro Evangelístico Church grew steadily over the years and became one of Costa Rica's first megachurches. Despite the resistance of other faith traditions (including other branches of Protestantism), Pentecostal churches are the ones that have experienced the most growth since the sixties in terms of number of churches planted, missions opened, and membership.[23]

An article by Universidad de Costa Rica's paper, *Semanario Universidad*, presented a study which compares data from 2019 and 2021. In such a short period of time some interesting changes happened concerning the Costa Rican religious landscape. According to the article, nonbelievers are on the rise; in just a year and half the number went from 19.9 percent to 27 percent. There also seems to be a slight reduction of Evangelicals which moved from 21.6 percent to 19.8 percent, but the difference is within the study's margin of error; meanwhile, Catholicism reached a historical new low: 47.5 percent.[24]

In my opinion, the fact that these changes happened during the pandemic does not follow that the changes happened because of the pandemic; nevertheless, one cannot rule out the possibility that the worldwide COVID crisis was a catalytic factor for

22. Yoder, "Fundamentalism and the Church," 48.
23. Holland, *Historia de la Iglesia Evangélica*, 26.
24. Murillo, "Encuesta CIEP-UCR Evidencia."

Deconstruction Is Not a Method

tendencies present long before. Writing back in 2015 for a theological and socioreligious Costa Rican journal, Dr. Laura Fuentes Belgrave identified a trend that had already been going on for a while: Costa Rican nonpracticing Catholics were—and still are—on the rise.[25] Fuentes Belgrave anticipated a generational change in which evangelical Christians and nonbelievers would revoke Catholic dominion of the religious field. In fact, the two main causes for Costa Ricans to become evangelical believers are either conversion or family lineage, in that order. The fact that family heritage is becoming such a significant factor in evangelical growth shows evangelical faith is emerging as an integrator for the national community on par with Catholicism.[26] It is important to note that more than 60 percent of the Costa Rican evangelical movement is comprised by Pentecostal Christians.[27]

Catholicism has had more success among the college educated than Evangelicalism. Most Catholics, either practicing or nonpracticing, have college level education; while most practicing Evangelicals have not finished high school and the more educated Evangelicals tend to be the nonpracticing ones. At this point it is important to clarify Costa Rica has a 97.9 percent literacy rate among its general population and a 99.4 percent among the youth population; in both cases female literacy rate is 0.1 percent higher.[28] This makes Costa Rica's overall population a fairly educated one. Among both Catholics and Evangelicals, the least practicing Christians are the younger ones.[29]

What lies on the other side of conservative Christianity? According to Marcus Borg, on the opposite side of conservative Christianity we find progressive Christianity (he would locate most nonpracticing Christians in between both extremes). Most progressives can be found in mainline churches or living their religious lives independently from church. He recognizes progressives

---

25. Fuentes Belgrave, "Cambios en las Creencias Religiosas," 54.
26. Fuentes Belgrave, "Cambios en las Creencias Religiosas," 56–59.
27. Holland, *Análsis de la Obra Evangélica*, 11.
28. "Costa Rica."
29. Fuentes Belgrave, "Cambios en las Creencias Religiosas," 55.

are known more for what they do not believe (biblical inerrancy, literal interpretation, Jesus' death paid for human sin, and that Christianity is the exclusive way of salvation) than for what they actually affirm; therefore, Borg clarifies these affirmations: (1) The Bible is sacred Scripture to be interpreted historically and metaphorically; (2) salvation is primarily about transformation in this life; (3) the human predicament is that we find ourselves blind, diseased, and dead, living in the bondage of Egypt and the disconnection of exile; (4) Christ is not payment for human sin, Jesus, as the center of Christianity, reveals God's character and passion; (5) believing as understood in modern Christianity is merely an assertion of statements, while believing as understood in earlier Christianity was more about beloving, which has transformative power; and (6) Christianity is about a path of transformation, though this does not mean it is the only way to it.[30] Even when many conservative Christians might feel comfortable affirming most of these statements, in practice both conservative and progressives arrive to very different conclusions regarding issues like sexuality and cultural affirmation of Christian faith.

Churches that are constructed around the logic of binaries such as evangelical/catholic, capitalism/socialism, male/female (referring to ministry opportunities), pro-life/pro-choice, conservative/progressive will result in places of exclusion not just for those in the opposite extreme of the binary, but also for the many located in-between the extremes. Unlike the United States, mainline churches have not grown as much in Costa Rica; when summed up, Lutherans, Presbyterians, and Anglicans represent only 2.1 percent of all churches in the country.[31] This means that believers who don't agree with conservative Christianity have limited options: being effectively left out of congregational life, keeping silence in their evangelical congregations, or planting new congregations by themselves. But if the Costa Rican church learns to deconstruct in a healthy manner, it will also learn how to deal with a plurality of voices in welcoming and constructive ways.

30. Borg, *Convictions*, 14–16.
31. Holland, *Análisis de la Obra Evangélica*, 12.

Instead of closing down defensively or "watering down beliefs," the church can develop in its engagement with the current context.

Peter in the House of Cornelius: The Methodology of the Law

The unsettling vision Peter experienced instinctively awakens his reliance on known methods: "The law says no, therefore I cannot." This is a man who saw Jesus apply the law in the way it was originally intended: for the benefit of the sons and daughters of Abraham; yet his mind could not fathom that God could raise up children of Abraham even out of stones (Luke 7:8). The grace Christ extended to the Jews could not possibly be extended to the gentiles in the same way; the Holy Spirit that Christ poured over the sons and daughters of Abraham could not possibly fill the gentiles in the same way. This belief, this attitude towards his known methodologies is what the vision was uncovering.

Commenting on Peter's experience, Willimon says, "Faith . . . is our often breathless attempt to keep up with the redemptive activity of God, to keep asking ourselves, 'What is God doing?' . . . The wind has again blown where it wills (John 3:8), and now the church must account for its movements."[32] The Spirit is always moving, and the church should always respond accordingly. Methods are useful guides, but they also provide limiting perspectives. Ultimately the church must decide whether to be faithful to a method or to the moving of the Spirit; each has its place, but they do not share the same authority.

Pentecostal Perspective: Affective-Narrative Epistemologies, Beyond Methods

Caputo's description of deconstruction as *a way of thinking* is also the perfect description for Pentecostalism; it truly is *a way of thinking*: ever-expecting, ever-attentive to what God the Holy Spirit is

---

32. Willimon, *Acts*, 99.

doing. Albrecht and Howard identify two Pentecostal sensibilities relevant to this conversation: (1) orientation to experience, a "sensitivity built into the Pentecostal mind and heart;" and (2) attention to the Holy Spirit, leading to "an affective ability to notice the nuances of the Spirit."[33]

Because of these sensibilities, Pentecostals have defied the evangelical tendency of giving preference to the work of the apostle Paul and instead have naturally gravitated towards the narrative genres found in the Gospels and Acts.[34] This is one of the reasons Pentecostals have developed what Smith calls "an affective, narrative epistemology"; he explains, "Narrative knowledge is found in the connection between narratives and emotions.... A 'logic' that is not deductive but affective.... It is emotive.... The emotions are themselves already 'construals' of the world."[35] Such epistemology explains why testimony is central to Pentecostal spirituality.

Just like Peter who was filled with the Spirit in Acts 2 but was hindered in God's mission by his persistent overreliance on the methods of the law, so has it happened to the Pentecostal church in many places of Latin America, Costa Rica included. A church unquestionably filled with the Spirit of God has relied too much on the methods of Fundamentalism and is now being hindered in its pursuit of God's mission. The church that supposedly makes room for the Spirit to lead has mistaken the voice of God for the voice of modernity's Fundamentalism.

In *Erring*, Mark C. Taylor mentions how postmodern thinkers revealed that "what for centuries had been regarded as objective reality is, in fact, subjective projection. Inverting the traditional Creator/creature relation, God came to be regarded as the creation of human beings."[36] It is easy to believe that such blame could only be assigned to scientific methods, but in fact, Fundamentalism allows the creatures to keep the Creator under control, out of Cornelius's house, by the convenient reliance on excluding binaries (to

---

33. Albrecht and Howard, "Pentecostal Spirituality," 241.
34. Wariboko and Yong, *Paul Tillich and Pentecostal Theology*, 7.
35. Smith, "Thinking in Tongues," 65.
36. Taylor, *Erring*, 4.

Deconstruction Is Not a Method

mention one example). Taylor continues to explain that the history of Western religion can be described as a pendular move between "seemingly exclusive and evident opposites"; constantly swinging back and forth between concepts like God and world, being and becoming, transcendent and immanent, mind and matter, height and depth, and so on.[37]

The ever-present danger of correcting one's path is to simply fall into a pendular movement of extremes. Even more, the pendular movement might be so hard that it thrusts some people outside of the faith to a movement from belief to atheism. This of course is modern language since the concept of atheism as we know it is a modern development; nevertheless, the New Testament testifies there have always been people within the community of faith who have "rejected and so have suffered shipwreck with regard to the faith" (1 Tim 1:19 NIV). Zahnd identifies such movement as demolition rather than deconstruction; in his experience this happens many times because people remain fundamentalist at their core, meaning they move from Christian Fundamentalism to atheistic Fundamentalism.[38] Enns talks about "the sin of certainty," which occurs when the need to be right fueled by fear is what guides our life of faith; this leads us to trust more in our mental images of God (which can become idols) than trusting God himself to help us grow in our knowledge and relationship to him. People who assume this posture live a faith marked by stress, anxiety, belligerence, pride, constant monitoring of others; but in the end, is more about fear than faith.[39] When fear fuels a life people can live this way either from within Christian faith or from atheism.

Deconstruction is more about managing tensions than it is about resolving them. Sometimes the Spirit takes us to the house of Cornelius, where tensions abound and methodologies fail, but it is there where we are challenged to abandon our fears and embrace a living faith.

---

37. Taylor, *Erring*, 8.
38. Zahnd, *When Everything's on Fire*, 26–27.
39. Enns, *Sin of Certainty*, 18–19, 204–5.

5

Deconstruction Is a Call

> *"Justice is what gives us the impulse, the drive, or the movement to improve the law, that is, to deconstruct the law. . . . The condition of possibility of deconstruction is a call for justice."*[1]
>
> —J. Derrida

BY USING THE THEME of justice, Derrida is explaining an important feature of deconstruction: it is fueled by, and always after, an unconditional. In *Force of Law* he is after the ideal of justice, in *Rogues* he searches for the ideal of democracy, in *Of Hospitality* he pursues the ideal of hospitality, and so on. From his perspective humans give conditioned expressions to unconditional ideals, so the human experience is a continual, never-ending search for that which is unconditioned.

Therefore, "the mark of the human condition is to live *in the distance between the conditional and unconditional*, to constantly

---

1. Caputo, *Deconstruction in a Nutshell*, 16.

Deconstruction Is a Call

negotiate between them."[2] In this sense, deconstruction could be thought of as a circular movement but not one forever entrapped in the same discussions. Deconstruction recognizes there is an undecidability in the midst of *différance* (the overlapping matrices of meaning), but it still responds without vacillation or postponement, fully aware of its imperfect response, always open to growth. Thus, perhaps a more accurate conception of deconstruction would be thinking about it as an upward spiral, always reaching beyond, always working toward shortening the distance between the conditional and the unconditional. Just like we are always running after justice, democracy, or hospitality but still never quite arriving at their full expression, understanding that "no construction can ever be adequate to the undeconstructible and so every construction stands under constant judgement by the undeconstructible."[3] Deconstruction, then, does not seek anarchy but responsibility to the undeconstructible, ever after the calling of the unconditional which is deconstruction's only true allegiance.

According to Heidegger any call asks three questions; Caputo answers them from the perspective of deconstruction as follows:[4]

1. *Who or what is being called upon?* We are the ones called upon.

2. *Who or what is being called for?* The calling is for the fulfillment of the promises made by the traditions and institutions we have inherited, those who first assumed the impossible task of constructing a representation of the undeconstructible.

---

2. Caputo, *Hoping against Hope*, 37. Going back to the ideas from the last chapter, note the inescapability, usefulness, and problems of binaries to express ideas. Once the binary unconditional/conditional has been constructed, the unconditional receives the privileged position, rightly so; but in practice this would mean that whoever *claims* to be closer to the unconditional will enjoy or assume a more privileged position in an argument.

3. This is what Caputo calls Derrida's "Jewish Principle" (*semper deconstruenda*, as described above) inspired by Tillich's "Protestant Principle" (*semper reformanda*: nothing finite and conditional can ever be adequate to the infinite and unconditional); Caputo, *Folly of God*, 31.

4. Caputo, *Folly of God*, 87–88.

3. *Who or what is calling?* God, who is the Unconditional event.[5] Nevertheless, it is important to note that in Caputo's theology God is not the Supreme Being of metaphysics because, according to him, such an idea is just one more product of *différance* (the interwoven matrices of meaning), a product which leads to dangerous militant theism. For him, "God" is an event that calls us even when it doesn't exist.[6] This conception is key for Caputo's differentiation between his proposed deconstructive "weak theology" and traditional apophatic theology. For him, even when both sound alike at some points the crucial difference is that the apophatic or mystical is intended as a doxology to "the highest of the high and the deepest of the deep."[7] Caputo is emphatic in stating that God, the unconditional, "does not exist; it insists . . . [even when] it is not a highest being, or even the ground of beings, or the hyper-being of apophatic tradition."[8] This idea is what gives Caputo the leverage to say that confessional bodies "do not know to whom they are praying . . . their confessional response to the call is but one of many possible responses to a call of ambiguous provenance."[9]

For Derrida, the call spooks the present with both ghosts from the past (*les revenants*) and ghosts from the future (*les arrivants*); this is the reason Caputo explains deconstruction as a *hauntology*[10] (a haunto-theology) that saves the old Ebenezer Scrooge through the terrifying ghosts of past and present. The Unconditional calls; we decide how to respond.

---

5. For Caputo, events are "what happens." Humans assign imperfect names to try to describe these uncontainable events, which is why a single event may receive many names; nevertheless, a name can never control that which it is trying to explain. See Stofanik, "Introduction to the Thinking," 20.

6. Caputo, *Hoping against Hope*, 107, 118, 122.

7. Caputo, *Folly of God*, 69–70.

8. Caputo, *Folly of God*, 34.

9. Caputo, *Folly of God*, 50.

10. Caputo, *Deconstruction in a Nutshell*, xxvii; see also Caputo, *Folly of God*, 30.

Deconstruction Is a Call

It is not in my interest to advocate for Caputo's theology; what I find useful is his perspective on what deconstruction is and how it works. I think we can learn from him and Derrida without necessarily espousing their theology; in fact, just because someone is deconstructing does not entail they would end up necessarily sharing their theological conclusions. That said, a person deconstructing can end up even further away from orthodoxy or much closer to it. I'll address the factors that can make a difference further on.

Costa Rican Context: Lived Spiritualities, the Response to a Call

Many Costa Rican believers are responding to a call from God as best as they can given the current circumstances. When we take a closer look at actual practices of Christian believers in Costa Rica, we find they are indeed indifferent to certain beliefs by simply overlooking some doctrinal principles; nevertheless, there is an actual tendency towards a *bricolage*: a personal reelaboration of religious beliefs.[11] Even when this phenomenon might not be ideal to some, I think it demonstrates there is still a deep spiritual hunger among many people. *Bricolage* religion is nothing new: "People have always mixed institutional religion with forms of popular piety"; the sacred and the profane have always existed in one way or another as a form of spiritual self-expression.[12]

For example, archeological discoveries from ancient Israelite sites have found not only amulets of the Egyptian dwarf-god Bes, but even manufacturing molds exposing the fact that these amulets were not just imported from other regions but they were also produced locally. The appeal of Bes was probably due to the fact that it was understood to be a guardian of newborns; even when Israelite women probably were not Bes worshipers, they could still find value in the amulets because visual symbols can

---

11. Fuentes Belgrave, "Cambios en las Creencias Religiosas," 53.
12. Campbell, "Relationship Between Religion," 79.

migrate across cultures while retaining their symbolic power and not necessarily their theological meaning.[13] Findings such as these harmonize with the biblical text, which continually cautions the Israelites against the dangers of idolatry, shining a light to a reality many pastors are familiar with: the way in which believers live their religious lives on a personal level is not always—perhaps even rarely—orthodox. A bricolage spirituality is not interested so much in theological coherence as it is in "spirituality coherence,"[14] an expression of religious life as understood by an individual who appropriates a diverse set of beliefs and practices.

For Campbell and others, the internet has played an important role in the development of heterogeneous faith, especially by giving visibility to mixing practices of different sources that used to be on the fringes of organized religion.[15] The internet is just one aspect of what Rainie and Wellman identify as a triple revolution that is comprised by the internet, social networks, and mobile devices; it has made possible what the authors call "networked individuals." These networked individuals are people who "have partial membership in multiple networks and rely less on permanent memberships in settled groups."[16] It follows that a believer who is exposed to this triple revolution will not understand herself as purely Pentecostal, Lutheran, or other but probably as someone who attends a Pentecostal church while also incorporating Catholic practices, yoga, nutrition, and a variety of ethical decisions as part of her lived spirituality. This networked individual will probably not care if her denomination sanctions these practices and beliefs or not.

Fuentes Belgrave's investigation in the Costa Rican context shows that the result of less religious practice is a greater re-elaboration of beliefs and a higher possibility to develop an "autonomous conscience."[17] This leads to a lay morality that shows disparities

---

13. Meyers, *Rediscovering Eve*, 155.
14. McKnight, "Spirituality in a Postmodern Age," 211.
15. Campbell, "Relationship Between Religion," 79.
16. Rainie and Wellman, *Networked*, 12.
17. Fuentes Belgrave, "Cambios en las Creencias Religiosas," 58.

Deconstruction Is a Call

between what religious leaders preach and what lay believers belief and practice.[18] This lay morality seems to be selective; for example, 55 percent of Costa Ricans think abortion should be a personal decision regarding every woman, while an equal percentage rejects adoption by same-sex couples.[19] Perhaps this shows our society is undergoing a cultural transition.

Even when Fuentes Belgrave does not define the concept "autonomous conscience," what she probably means is that said conscience is independent from a given religious organization. If she meant "autonomous" simply as an individualistic, self-sufficient accomplishment, she would be naively idealizing the autonomy of the individual in a modernistic fashion. Rainie and Wellman assume the postmodern posture when they analyze the networked individual: "[People] think they make choices independently of others. We may think we are free agents, but there are others whose presence in our networks and broader environments shapes the decisions we make."[20] This means the location of believing individuals is crucial in the elaboration of said beliefs. This location not only encompasses time and space, but the different networks the person inhabits. The role of the triple revolution in the development of faith is especially relevant in Costa Rica, a country that occupies second place in internet use in all of Latin America and where eight out of every ten people have internet access,[21] even if said access is not ideal, as the 2020 pandemic exposed.

The theory of the "networked individual" who has a partial membership yet remains influenced by these multiple networks appears to be true in the Costa Rican context. Costa Rican practicing Catholics and practicing Evangelicals declare to be highly influenced by religious leaders in their daily lives, but even many nonpracticing Evangelicals admit remaining highly influenced by religious leaders.[22] Another interesting bit of data shows that

---

18. Fuentes Belgrave, "Cambios en las Creencias Religiosas," 65.
19. Murillo, "Encuesta CIEP-UCR Evidencia."
20. Rainie and Wellman, *Networked*, 38.
21. "Estas Serán las Grandes Tendencias."
22. Fuentes Belgrave, "Cambios en las Creencias Religiosas," 65.

while almost all religious practices are weakening in the general population of Costa Rica, prayer is the one practice privileged by most. This may be because one's prayer life takes place in a private context in which the believer decides when, where, and how it happens.[23] Costa Ricans are not necessarily losing their faith as such but are decidedly changing their religious habits. The evidence is pointing us to the reality that pastors should find ways to minister to those who are on the fringes of faith institutions while still making space for the pastoral voice; otherwise, we might waste the real opportunities of ministry while waiting for the ideal ones.

It is clear that Costa Ricans seem to be responding to a call that is reconfiguring their religious practices and beliefs, but it would be naive to say that any voice who calls is God's; after all, the postmodern realization that we are immersed in multiple matrices of meaning or networks of influence also means we are exposed to a multiplicity of voices calling for our attention. The cultivation of discernment will be one of the key challenges for the church in this context. God is calling, but many other voices are calling, too.

Peter in the House of Cornelius: The Call

Peter discovered there is uncertainty when the Unconditional calls. The voice of the Spirit directs him to follow three strangers into an unknown context. Once the apostle arrives, Cornelius confirms Peter's prejudice: the ignorant gentile starts worshiping the apostle. After that awkward moment is dealt with, Peter little by little finds that the voice of the Unconditional calls whom he pleases in the way he pleases. Central to this Spirit-led experience is the revelation of what it means to call Jesus "Lord of all"; according to Willimon this is a "theological statement gleaned from the experience and faith of the apostles, not something to be proved from the Torah or prophets."[24] This phrase is used to highlight the instant shock of Peter's overwhelming experience; surely in Luke's

---

23. Fuentes Belgrave, "Cambios en las Creencias Religiosas," 61.
24. Willimon, *Acts*, 97–98.

mind there was a relationship between Peter's experience and Hebrew Scripture. Willimon clarifies we should not chase cultural trends in search of new revelation, but "we are continuing to penetrate the significance of scriptural witness that Jesus is Lord and to be faithful to divine prodding."[25]

There is always a disorienting factor when a new voice calls or when we are called in a new way by an already known voice. In order to allow motion, there needs to be some shaking of the foundations (which does not necessarily imply an abandonment of these). By following the voice of this call, Peter's beliefs were deconstructed by the Spirit into a deeper, richer understanding of orthodoxy, through an experiential encounter with God that, from a Christian perspective, harmonized with the Scriptures in previously unforeseen ways.

Pentecostal Perspective: Discernment in a World of Multiple Voices

As mentioned before, a distinctive Pentecostal sensitivity is the special attention to the Holy Spirit, "an affective ability to notice the nuances of the Spirit";[26] another of these sensitivities becomes relevant in this conversation, namely, a sense of spiritual warfare. Pentecostals believe there is a cosmic conflict, and the Spirit has empowered the church to be active participants in Christ's victory. When put together, these two sensitivities show the relevance of the Spirit's gift of discernment of spirits (1 Cor 12:10); we could also say discernment of voices.

To cultivate a discerning heart is a challenge for a networked individual whose overexposure to information might lead him to believe he has found wisdom; whose overstimulated brain might find it very hard to engage in silence, solitude, and prayer; and whose unhealthy need for immediacy might preclude him from taking the time discernment demands.

---

25. Willimon, *Acts*, 99.
26. Albrecht and Howard, "Pentecostal Spirituality," 241.

Deconstruction and the Spirit

Discernment is not an individualistic revelation but a communal exercise. First Corinthians frames it within the context of the body. In fact, when a prophet speaks, the church is not called to be a passive recipient but an active participant by judging that voice (1 Cor 14:29). Calls demand discernment because God is not the only one who calls. Ignatian spirituality, which is highly charismatic, teaches that good and evil spirits operate in opposing ways: good spirits work in light and openness, producing love, joy, and peace; evil spirits work cloaked with secrecy and deception, producing confusion, doubt, and disgust.[27]

Teaching how to develop a discerning heart produces mature disciples who are able to follow the call into God's mission in new and daring ways. Kinnaman and Matlock talk about the importance of cultivating cultural discernment, defined as "the ability to compare beliefs, values, customs, and creations of the world we live in (digital Babylon) to those of the world we belong to (the kingdom of God)."[28] Teaching cultural discernment demands becoming "robust learning communities"[29] where critical thinking is taught and encouraged, even if that means challenging supposedly prophetic voices. While Fuentes Belgrave's study showed that the less a believer engages in religious practice, the greater reelaboration of beliefs, Peter experienced a reelaboration of beliefs by faithfully engaging in Christian practice; both engagement and disengagement can lead to reelaborations, probably different ones. The church should be a community where deconstructive experiences are nurtured by a mature discerning community. In the end, Christian discernment is not simply about decision-making; it is about faithfulness to God amid a multivocal world.

---

27. Tetlow, "Discernment in a Nutshell."
28. Kinnaman and Matlock, *Faith for Exiles*, 74.
29. Kinnaman and Matlock, *Faith for Exiles*, 93.

6

Deconstruction Is a "Yes" to the Other

"Deconstruction is 'yes,' is linked to the 'yes,' is an affirmation. . . . When I say 'yes' to the other, in the form of a promise or an agreement or an oath, the 'yes' must be absolutely inaugural."[1]

—J. Derrida

JACQUES DERRIDA WAS AN outsider, a "European without quite being European, French without being French, Jewish without being Jewish, Algerian without being Algerian."[2] Watkin has the sensibility to warn us against reducing Derrida to his biography, acknowledging Derrida's own discomfort at this idea; yet, at this point I find it relevant to echo some of Watkin's brief biographical remarks, showing Derrida was indeed "the other" who was told "no" plenty of times at a fairly young age.

1. Caputo, *Deconstruction in a Nutshell*, 27.
2. Caputo, *Deconstruction in a Nutshell*, 114.

Deconstruction and the Spirit

Derrida was born in the city of El Biar, Algeria, at a time when it was officially part of France. While he was in school, it was customary that the top-of-the-class students would have the honor of raising the French flag, but because he was a Jew under a Nazi-sympathizing regime, Derrida was not only denied this honor but was eventually expelled.[3] He would later describe himself as a "little black and very Arab Jew"[4] and an "over-acculturated, over-colonized European hybrid."[5] It makes a lot of sense that after experiencing the ethical failures of modernity he would deem it important to say "yes to the other."

Deconstruction raises an eyebrow before expressions such as "we" or "our," for these suggest a group shares a particular historical experience;[6] words like "community" imply a harmony and consensus that do not necessarily exist between insiders while simultaneously assuming defensive postures toward outsiders. Deconstruction, on the other hand, is porous, open to the other, and never defensive; it is not afraid of people being different; it thrives on dissimilarities. For Derrida the problem we face is not relativism; things are not relative but incommensurable, making it impossible to do justice to them if we dare to compare. What incommensurability means is that "every other is wholly other";[7] and if we fail to respect this singularity, we are acting violently towards the other; paradoxically, as expected in deconstruction, we cannot completely avoid this violence. Yet, as we have learned, deconstruction is constantly after the impossible.

One way of saying no to the other is through the protection afforded by traditions, when we allow "the first reading [to] become the last word."[8] Deconstruction defends the tension between dominant and transgressive readings of the great traditions, while conservatism seeks to solve this tension by always going back to

3. Watkin, *Jacques Derrida*, 1–2.
4. Derrida and Bennington, *Circumfession*, 51.
5. Derrida, *Other Heading*, 7.
6. See Derrida, *Points de Suspension*, 366.
7. Watkin, *Jacques Derrida*, 29–35.
8. Caputo, *Deconstruction in a Nutshell*, 79, 81.

the classical reading. The challenge of every community is retaining its own identity while remaining open to outsiders. So, instead of community, deconstruction prefers to talk about hospitality: welcoming the stranger. This kind of hospitality resists the temptation of being limited or, even worse, degrading into welcoming the same while being hostile to the stranger;[9] an impossible kind of hospitality that "does not come down to knowing anything, but to doing something,"[10] just like deconstruction itself.

Costa Rican Context: Globalization and Pluralism, When the "Yes to the Other" Is Not Reciprocal

Globalization is a broad and complex concept, but social theorists in general agree that it "refers to fundamental changes in the spatial and temporal contours of social existence, according to which the significance of space or territory undergoes shifts in the face of a no less dramatic acceleration in the temporal structure of crucial forms of human activity."[11] The basic components of globalization are (1) deterritorialization, a multiplicity of social activities increasingly takes place regardless of the physical location of partakers; (2) interconnectedness across boundaries permitting distant forces to impact local and regional events; (3) an acceleration of crucial forms of social activity; (4) a long-term process with nonuniversal and varying degrees of impact; (5) a multipronged process whose effects can be seen in culture, economy, politics, and other aspects of life.

The influence of this phenomenon is strongly felt in the Global South. "It has become the single most powerful narrative reshaping the economies of the world, national identities, and social relationships between peoples."[12] Roxburgh calls it a

9. See Caputo, *Deconstruction in a Nutshell*, 108–10 and Caputo, *Folly of God*, 63.
10. Caputo, *Deconstruction in a Nutshell*, 112.
11. Scheuerman, "Globalization," para. 2.
12. Roxburgh, *Missional Map-Making*, 90.

secular theology because it offers an alternative vision of salvation and eschaton; the market is given the power to unite and renew the world. Of course, it demands the offering of lives to submit to its "around-the-world, around-the-clock" markets, making it difficult for individuals to have other priorities such as family or church. One can see the challenge for nurturing the kind of spirituality that seeks to remain constantly open to the direction of the Holy Spirit; an around-the-clock job does not leave room or energy for contemplation.

Costa Rica's high level of literacy has placed the country in an ideal place to participate in globalization allowing big names like Microsoft, Kimberly-Clark, Marriott, Four Seasons, Intel, Hewlett-Packard, Amazon, and many others to find a highly skilled workforce while receiving many benefits from the government that local businesses do not receive. Of course, they are also in a position to provide many benefits to the employees that local businesses cannot provide.

Globalization also provides great opportunities for the global church to exert its influence around the world. Believers can communicate and travel to many different places while living out their faith in professional circles. This can represent a challenge, yet is possible. Ministries and missionaries can find easier access to communication and travel; because of global interconnectedness, cooperation between local ministries from around the world has never been easier.

Nevertheless, globalization can also turn out to be just another form of imperialism.[13] The first step to participate of global salvation is learning the English language and with it different forms of enculturation. Older generations perceive huge cultural differences when engaging in a globalized world, while new generations naturally adopt the new reality as part of their identity. This change allows them unprecedented cross-cultural agility, but the newly developed identity can also hinder them from connecting to their roots. In the long run, a new culture distinctly defined by the dominant one is being created.

13. Jenkins, *Next Christendom*, 16.

Deconstruction Is a "Yes" to the Other

Globalization and pluralism are related but in constant tension, many times even in conflict; while the latter promotes a vision of a universal Western framework, the former envisions "a world in which no single power exercises hegemony and no single belief or ideology dominates."[14] Many cultures which appeared to be monolithic are exposed to other customs and beliefs, making the pluralistic phenomenon either an enriching experience that provides new perspectives or a disorienting loss that menaces identity. Either way, the pluralistic culture invites people into bricolage faith; understanding doctrines as points of view and experimenting with fragments of other traditions and religions to find whatever suits one's lifestyle.

Migration also presents challenges regarding pluralism. Costa Rica is the only country in the Central American region with a positive value of net migration, meaning there are more people coming than those leaving.[15] Most immigrants come from Nicaragua trying to find jobs and better opportunities; many others come fleeing Venezuela's crisis; but there are also plenty of immigrants who come for tourism, education, and business (not always with best intentions, there is a big human trafficking problem in the country), which means Costa Ricans are exposed on a regular basis to a wide range of ideas and lifestyles from places such as Asia, Europe, and North America.

The effects of globalization as imperialism are evidenced by the power differentials between global relationships. Once a person gets her voice "out there," she'll find out the volume assigned to each voice is not necessarily equal, or at least not heard in the same way. A common challenge for Latin American theologians, for example, is that they do not do theology like Westerners; they do "Latin American theology." Jenkins narrates the encounter a leader from the Global South had with a leader from a mainstream Western denomination; the Westerner said with contempt, "Your beliefs are too young"; the comeback from the Global South leader was noteworthy: "All heresies emanated from you, have flourished

---

14. Roxburgh, *Missional Map-Making*, 94.
15. "Migración Neta—Costa Rica."

among you; by us, that is by the Southern nations, they have been here strangled, here put an end to." Jenkins also recognizes the general disdain academics have towards Pentecostalism and anything related to Fundamentalism.[16] It is in this climate that we, Latin American Pentecostals, look toward the future from the Global South trying to find the ways in which we should serve global Christianity.

There is also a set of expectations from Western churches over Global South churches, especially from ministries in the United States where *tico*[17] ministries have cultivated a lot of connections historically. Both liberals and conservatives project their expectations toward Latin American ministries, liberals because of the region's strong attraction towards socialism, conservatives because of the long history of conservatism in the area. Will there be any room for Costa Rican ministries to define their global identities? What would happen if *tico* ministries do not comply to foreign expectations? Will Costa Rican voices be canceled by liberals or conservatives? Will resources be held back? Just imagine gentile churches holding back their offerings because of their differences with the church in Jerusalem! How much room will Costa Rican Pentecostals be given by religious forces to influence worldwide Christianity? Would it just come to a matter of getting enough critical mass not to be ignored? The rules in order to get a seat at the global table are neither uniform nor universal.

The famed postmodern openness to religion can be very selective. It is still very much influenced by modernity's belief in reason and reliance on the material world. There appears to be a certain fear of not being believed by the modern project. I think Caputo's ideas about a metaphysical God (which follow after Tillich's thoughts) show this: "God insists, but God does not exist";[18] "the folly of the kingdom of God does not need God. In

---

16. Jenkins, *Next Christendom*, 258, 271.

17. An affectionate way to say "Costa Ricans," it comes from the Costa Rican longstanding tendency to use diminutives, e.g. *chiquitico* (tiny), *cositico* (little thing), *llenitico* (completely full).

18. Caputo, *Folly of God*, 77–76.

Deconstruction Is a "Yes" to the Other

fact, the Supreme Being would ruin everything";[19] "everything we say about God is symbolic";[20] and "the mythological sets in when we literalize the symbolic, when we forget that the symbol is a symbol."[21] So, Caputo proposes the idea of a nonpersonal God assuming a kind of apologetic posture while trying to transcend the theist-atheist debate; the following unfortunate paragraph gives context to his concern:

> Religion, with its unrelenting supernaturalism and mythologizing, is making itself more and more unbelievable and is seeing to it that belief flourishes best among the most deprived and desperate, the poorest and the most undereducated people on the globe, while finding itself increasingly irrelevant to everyone else. . . . Once an individual or a culture reaches a certain stage of intellectual clarity and economic stability, even after centuries of doctrinal servitude, its religious beliefs become, well, unbelievable and incur mass incredulity. . . . [This] is beginning to happen among the growing middle class in South America.[22]

As a Latin American I cannot help but feel like Caputo shares the same intellectual sense of superiority as those atheists (not all) who look down on people who believe there is a God. While writing a book devoted to *The Folly of God*, Caputo rejects the ideas others might have about God, treating them as too foolish (uneducated). Deconstruction is about openness to the other, the other being "the outsider, the enemy, the weak and hurting, the person in need, the powerless and homeless";[23] nevertheless, this posture from Caputo seems quite closed to the *other* church, the church in the Global South which is "quite at home with biblical notions of the supernatural."[24] His expression sounds like there really is no

19. Caputo, *Folly of God*, 112.
20. Caputo, *Folly of God*, 15.
21. Caputo, *Folly of God*, 17.
22. Caputo, *Folly of God*, 76.
23. Olson, *Journey of Modern Theology*, 693.
24. Jenkins, *Next Christendom*, 273.

place for the *other* church in Western postmodernity, unless this *other* church embraces a totalizing narrative pushed by those with access to "real" knowledge and the privilege of deconstruction.

Caputo also seems to assume the decrease in number of practicing believers we are seeing in places with a strong middle class, such as Costa Rica, implies a preference for atheism or at least with finding the idea of a metaphysical higher being to be problematic, but in my experience, this is just not true. Most people who leave faith communities still hold a strong belief in the traditional concept of God.

This postmodern urge to be accepted by modern ideals can be seen in other authors such as Philip Gulley, who passionately envisions "an evolved Christianity [that] will not insist we believe the absurd" or "affirm the incredible."[25] The relationship between science and religion is an ongoing conversation, and I wholeheartedly share Gulley's longing for a church that will be a friend of science; our local church, for example, unambiguously promoted the use of masks and vaccines during the COVID pandemic, to the point of being a vaccination center for our city. Yet, along with most of my Latin American Pentecostal sisters and brothers, I do not believe a materialistic explanation of the universe is enough, and many believers around the world choose to proudly affirm along with Paul (and Caputo?) that there is folly, according to human standards, in following Christ. Perhaps Gulley would agree that a grace which is not absurd and a faith which is not incredible are probably not worth it.

Peter in the House of Cornelius: A "Yes" to the Other Believers

The Spirit is clearly working in Peter's heart to move him from a resounding "no" to the other believers to an embracing and sincere "yes." God's plan amazes the apostle. All along the divine was working towards the inclusion of all the world in Abraham's promise.

---

25. Gulley, *Evolution of Faith*, 8–9.

Deconstruction Is a "Yes" to the Other

A relationship between the Jewish apostle and the Roman centurion presented many challenges. Cornelius represented the imperial forces that subjugated Israel, but still he was devout! Peter represented the kingdom of God that reconciles the world to him, but still he would not sit at a gentile table! Both men were simultaneously at the center and at the fringes. Cornelius was at the center of political power but on the fringes of religion. Peter was at the center of the Christian community but on the fringes of political power. God stands in between both men to bring them together; both are invited to a mutual encounter orchestrated actively by the divine. Cornelius sincerely opened his home while Peter reluctantly accepted the invitation. In a way each man needs something the other has, but since the Spirit interrupts the apostle's speech, we could say the story is more about what the apostle learned than about what the centurion received from the apostle. In the end it was not the amazing, supernatural vision that transformed Peter in the privacy of prayer time, but a shared experience with those in the margins of religion during a God-designed encounter in which the apostle seems almost as a spectator.

We can now see what Justo González means about the church's expansion in Acts by setting borders, points of mutual encounter that led to *mestizaje* experiences. Willimon points out the dual nature of Peter and Cornelius's story; they both have a vision and make speeches because "both Cornelius and Peter need changing if God's mission is to go forward."[26] The call is framed by a purpose, opening up "joyous new possibilities for community."[27] God is the one saying "yes to the other"; the church follows his lead.

---

26. Willimon, *Acts*, 96.
27. Willimon, *Acts*, 97.

Pentecostal Perspective: Finding God in the Others

The Holy Spirit actively creates spaces for mutual human encounter within the divine. This is celebrated by the Pentecostal church in at least two ways.

First, Pentecostal spirituality is characterized by the value of participation.[28] The Spirit bestows gifts on each member of the church body in such a way that every person has something that someone else needs and a single person will always need something someone else has. The church comes together to minister to one another by freely giving what each believer freely received. This leads to a dynamic relationship between the corporate and the personal; the Spirit constantly speaks to individuals in private spaces so they can share and minister to the community, and the community expects and celebrates personal experiences. Pentecostal spirituality, then, bends towards the organic instead of the structure, so much so that Paul needs to structure Corinthian charismatic celebrations.

The Pentecostal awareness of the polycentric nature of the church is seen in how the movement has interpreted the roles described by Eph 4:11 as an ongoing reality. Local Pentecostal churches actively cultivate the development of people who can function as apostles, prophets, evangelists, pastors, and teachers because Christ keeps providing for his church through the Spirit. Even when there is still room to grow in this aspect in Latin America, healthy local Pentecostal leadership seeks to be polycentric, i.e., the constant interaction between a variety of anointed believers called to minister Christ's church.

A second aspect that positions Pentecostal spirituality to say "yes to the other" comes from its "eschatological orientation to mission and justice . . . expressed in terms of empowerment, with a preferential option for the marginalized."[29] This happens with a sense of urgency, because Pentecostalism wholly identifies with

---

28. Albrecht and Howard, "Pentecostal Spirituality," 243.
29. Smith, *Thinking in Tongues*, 12.

Deconstruction Is a "Yes" to the Other

the interpretation that the early church gave to the words uttered by the prophet Joel: the Spirit is poured by God "in the last days" (Acts 2:17). This eschatology "engenders a commitment to mission and to ministries of empowerment and social justice"[30] because the Pentecostal church understands clearly that the Spirit moves among those who "are not," as in Corinth.

One final thought on this point is that deconstruction should not just be sealed by a "yes to the other," but first and foremost a "yes to the Other," to the one who is calling. Pentecostal spirituality not only believes God insists, but that he also exists and wants a close relationship with his children while bringing them together in mutual encounter. The one who is calling deserves a response, saying "yes" to him will always lead us into a "yes to the other."

---

30. Smith, *Thinking in Tongues*, 45.

7

Deconstruction Is Affirmative of Institutions... Is Not Destruction

> "What is called deconstruction... has never, never opposed institutions as such.... I think that the life of an institution implies that we are able to criticize, to transform, to open the institution to its own future.... If an institution is to be an institution, it must to some extent break with the past, keep the memory of the past, while inaugurating something absolutely new."[1]
>
> —J. Derrida

HANS-GEORG GADAMER WAS A continental philosopher like Derrida who in 1960 published *Truth and Method*, a work which portrays his understanding of philosophical hermeneutics. Much à la Derrida, he understood his work more as a theory than a method.

---

1. Caputo, *Deconstruction in a Nutshell*, 5–6.

Deconstruction Is Affirmative of Institutions... Is Not Destruction

For him, tradition is what happens to us, we are immersed in it, we belong to history; we first understand ourselves and our world through contexts which provide us with prejudices.[2] According to Gadamer tradition provides a place to stand, making interpretation possible, but at the same time, it limits what we can see from that standpoint. He also recognizes we are formed by a plurality of traditions; in my case I was formed by the interaction of the Costa Rican tradition, the Pentecostal tradition, and the Christian tradition; all of these are at the same time made up by multiple streams of traditions (similar to Derrida's reasoning). Consequently, an infinite number of interpretations is possible, but this does not mean all interpretations will be valid or illuminating.[3]

Gadamer's insight that we belong to history is very important because it helps us appreciate that *traditions are identities*. These are not simply a set of ideas, customs, and habits. Traditions are an essential part of being human. Even if these traditions are to be challenged, Gadamer understands that they deserve our respect; as he notes, "the discovery that parental traditions are finite and fallible is not the discovery (1) that they are always wrong or (2) that we ourselves are somehow infinite and infallible."[4] To treat traditions with respect from a postmodern perspective means to recognize that even if their authority is not absolute, there may be truth within them.[5]

The *destruction* of religion is the "modern critical approach to religion"; the postmodern approach, on the other hand, is one of "repetition,"[6] but a kind of repetition that is more faithful to the Unconditional (God) than to tradition. Institutions are the champions of tradition. In the language of faith, institutions take the form of confessional religions. Even when these are seen as conditioned responses to the Unconditional according to deconstruction, still "that does not mean the confessional theologies are

---

2. Gadamer, *Truth and Method*, 277–78.
3. Westphal, *Whose Community? Which Interpretation?*, 71.
4. Westphal, *Whose Community? Which Interpretation?*, 75.
5. Westphal, *Whose Community? Which Interpretation?*, 75.
6. Caputo, *Hoping against Hope*, 19.

to be taken lightly or simply brushed aside."[7] Deconstruction is not against tradition but against conservatism; it seeks to keep tradition alive by forcing us to recognize the multiplicity within its history and demanding that we take responsibility for the traditions to which we hold on to.[8] Once again, we can see deconstruction is about maintaining tensions between a recognition of the past (fidelity) and the affirmation of the future (hope). Deconstruction is about memory as well as innovation.

Both Derrida and Caputo invested a good part of their lives in educational institutions, and none of them were ever accused of setting them on fire (at least in a literal way). Their praxis attests that deconstructionists do find value in institutions and can be an active part in building them. The book *Deconstruction in a Nutshell* exists precisely because Derrida and Caputo were inaugurating a new program at Villanova University, a Roman Catholic school.

Deconstruction is affirmative of institutions, not opposed to them. Deconstructionists are called to work within institutions for the benefit of these, out of faithfulness to the Unconditional. They continually affirm the truth found within the inherited traditions, while challenging the inherited misconceptions.

Costa Rican Context: Current Challenges for Institutions

The forces of globalization and pluralism are connected to the miracle of accelerated technological advances, "the shared experience of living in a highly technological era provides a universal ground for a pluralistic society."[9] Technology provides the center of gravity that pulls everything together. This global community is comprised by individuals who are quickly learning that technological savviness is rewarded with flexibility, autonomy, and authority.

---

7. Caputo, *Folly of God*, 49.
8. Caputo, *Deconstruction in a Nutshell*, 37; see also Caputo, *Folly of God*, 30.
9. Robinson, *Appletopia*, 104.

In this context independent thinking is not only an advantage, but also expected.

Many times, this reality is assumed uncritically because even when technology's power and influence is omnipresent in our daily lives, it is easy to overlook its effects. Theologian and producer Craig Detweiler meditates on the faith society places over technology:

> Our faith in technology is so pervasive it is often blind. . . . Our faith in technology is impatient. It does not tolerate delays. . . . Our faith in technology connects us to long lost friends. It also enables us to avoid people we'd rather text with than talk to. . . . Our faith in technology is so widespread that we feel we must be always available. . . . Our faith in technology is so complete that we place devices into our children's hands at earlier ages and stages. . . Our faith in technology is so passionate that we rarely question the wisdom of our embrace.[10]

Perhaps we could say technology is the promised messiah that will inaugurate globalization's eschaton, that which will finally bring salvation to humanity and save us even from ourselves. As Costa Rican society increasingly incorporates new technologies in daily life, we run the risk of placing our faith and hope in the idols of modernity. Detweiler reminds us of technology's transformational power not only affects our environment but also our inner world: "Our defining technologies tend to define us (and our beliefs)."[11] A good example is the idea of seeing God as a great Watchmaker and creation as the perfectly calibrated mechanism he set in motion. The influence technology exerts (whether we are aware of it or not) is altering *how* we believe, even *what* we believe. As our hearts get captured by technology, it would be wise to remember that *as we worship, so we live, so we believe*.[12]

Thanks to technology people no longer have to go to church in order to access resources traditionally managed by it: "The church's monopoly on Christian instruction is over. People feel quite free to

---

10. Detweiler, *iGods*, 1–2.
11. Detweiler, *iGods*, 25.
12. *Lex orandi, lex credendi, lex vivendi.*

Deconstruction and the Spirit

join in theological discourse without the buffer of the church or its clergy."[13] This allows them to also use unconventional resources next to the ones they are used to. Robinson reminds us technology has been democratizing religious ideas since the invention of the press, but the computer has decentralized these ideas like never before, producing a new internet-age ethic "rooted in free expression, a breakdown of hierarchy, a sense of individual empowerment, and a distrust of central authority."[14] The selfie generation has embraced the idea of a "personal relationship with Jesus," quite popular among evangelical circles, and has taken it to mean an "excluding relationship with Jesus" that disallows any opinion coming from others, especially formal authorities. For some people the notion of religious authority is tied with control of religious resources, affirming that "the authority of leaders diminishes when a medium allows different people to have open access and gain greater control over knowledge and social information."[15] However this is only true if authority is interpreted as control. The fact that controlling leaders are losing their grip over the monopoly of narratives and information is a positive trend, yet this kind of leadership is not a reflection of true New Testament models of authority which are kenotic[16] in nature.

In a context in which "structured and bounded organizations are becoming supplanted by more *ad hoc*, open, and informal networks of civic involvement and religious practice," how should churches function?[17] Paradoxically, the mistrust of formal authority happens alongside the illusion of intimacy with total strangers, created by shared spaces of conversation with people completely alien to a person's immediate context such as celebrities, influencers, politicians, and many others. Because of the spaces created

---

13. Gulley, *Evolution of Faith*, 5.
14. Robinson, *Appletopia*, 12.
15. Cheong, "Authority," 72.
16. Referring to the self-emptying attitude demonstrated in the incarnation of Christ as seen in Phil 2:7
17. Rainie and Wellman, *Networked*, 29.

by technology, those close to us are not worthy of our trust while strangers feel like friends.

A changing world demands transformation in how the exercise of ministry has been constructed. Hopefully, more than just adapting to changes, leaders will learn because they love those they are called to minister. In a tech-obsessed world, it makes a huge difference to assume a more egalitarian approach to ministry, honoring the priesthood of all believers, as well as a assuming a listening posture. Institutions need to be deconstructed and reconstructed for their own sake. The church as an institution should revise its methodologies.

Peter in the House of Cornelius: The Institutionalized Church of Acts

After such an amazing experience, Peter goes to the church in Jerusalem to explain what took place, initiating a conversation that would take several years. Even when some people who are suspicious of institutions point to the New Testament as witness to a more organic church, I think we can see that from the earliest days the church assumed some sort of institutional structure to which even the apostle Peter was held accountable. Institutions are not desks or budgets, Andy Crouch explains, "*institution* is the name that sociologists have given to any deeply and persistently organized pattern of human behavior"; institutions exist so something of value can be taken care of so generations to come can enjoy it and flourish.[18] The apostle's deconstructive experience did not detach him from the church; it was used to plant a seed that would bear fruit in the coming years.

Willimon notes how in this section Luke places several conversion stories in succession to symbolize groups of converts, which are the fulfillment of the promise that the gospel would reach the ends of the world. These are unexpected acts of divine

---

18. Crouch, *Playing God*, 169.

grace that point to new beginnings.[19] In these new beginnings, the Spirit never condemns the existence of an organizational structure in the church, even when it had to enter in heated discussions while trying to make sense of the new reality. The Spirit constantly breathes new life on such an institution, actively participating to the point that it could be said "it seemed good to the Holy Spirit and to us" (Acts 15:28 NIV).

Institutions do not (and should not) exist for the sake of institutions, but for the benefit of the people they were formed to serve. Yes, traditions should be acknowledged as forms of communal and personal identities, that contain ancient wisdom from which new generations can draw and grow; but of which they will also be held accountable.

Pentecostal Perspective: The Church as the Place Where Deconstruction Happens

In a chapter in *The Pedagogics of Unlearning*, Caputo addresses how deconstruction can be applied to the context of educational institutions. Caputo shows how these institutions should be the place where students are unsettled, disturbed, and provoked in ways they never imagined before; according to him Derrida "has in mind a positive idea of institutions as a scene of the event. Deconstruction is all about institutions—schools, hospitals, political bodies, courts, museums—and how to keep them in creative disequilibrium without tipping over."[20] The role of the teacher must be conceived as one who does not attempt to manipulate the event but one who works with a weak force, in a middle voice as a caretaker of the event, not its master. Caputo explicitly states, "The school must be the place in which the event is possible."[21] If this is true, then it is also true that *the church must be the place in which the event is possible.*

---

19. Willimon, *Acts*, 100–104.
20. Caputo, "Teaching the Event," 121.
21. Caputo, "Teaching the Event," 123.

Deconstruction Is Affirmative of Institutions... Is Not Destruction

In schools as places for the event there is a program for education, but this is not meant to program the student; there is actually room within the program to expose the student to chance and exploration of what may haunt the learning process.[22] This happens to be a very pneumatic posture. As Jesus was breaking new ground in a class with a highly advanced student, he introduced him to a similar idea: "The wind blows wherever it pleases. You hear its sound, but you cannot tell where it comes from or where it is going. So it is with everyone born of the Spirit" (John 3:8 NIV). Education in the local church must plan to expose believers to unexpected ideas and teach them to navigate the winds of the Spirit.

One of the ways in which Smith's "radical openness to God" manifests itself is what Albrecht and Howard identify as the Pentecostal value for *restoration*.[23] Pentecostalism understands itself as a radical restoration of God's dealing with humanity. Such restoration created a tension with traditional Christianity even when it was understood as gift for the whole church, something that Charismatic movements executed better.[24] Pentecostalism itself has been like Peter standing before the church in Jerusalem, calling for the restoration of the Spirit's movement at a global scale. At the same time we can expect "little Peters" to stand within their local Pentecostal churches, being a voice for restoration and Spirit-infused deconstruction at the local level.

As Caputo probably expects, schools will always need to teach methods, mathematical formulas, philosophical principles; but he also expects this to happen with a radical openness to new surprises. Then it is completely acceptable for churches to embrace "thick confessional identities . . . a generous orthodoxy and healthy catholicity," which is what Smith understands the work of Derrida, Lyotard, and Foucault is calling the church to.[25] Pentecostal discipleship should

---

22. Caputo, "Teaching the Event," 126.
23. Smith, *Thinking in Tongues*, 12.
24. Albrecht and Howard, "Pentecostal Spirituality," 247.
25. Smith, *Who's Afraid of Postmodernism*, 117, 132, 143. See also the seminal work of radical orthodoxy by Milbank, *Theology and Social Theory*, as well as Milbank et al., *Radical Orthodoxy: A New Theology*.

Deconstruction and the Spirit

embrace this "radical orthodoxy" while also remaining radically open to the move of the Spirit, who comes to renew his church by affirming us into deeper orthodoxy while confronting human-made constructions that hinder the church's mission.

Pentecost was the celebration of the law being given to Moses at Mount Sinai, the most orthodox moment, but now it was presented in a new way to the Christian church, the coming of the Spirit in a new season. This is what Caputo would call the balance between the *ruly* and the *unruly*, where deconstruction thrives. With Pentecost in mind Wariboko proposes the Pentecostal principle: "The capacity to begin. It encapsulates the notion that no finite or conditioned reality can claim to have reached its destiny. . . . Every end has only one option: to be a new beginning."[26] May the church be a place of amazement, new beginnings, and a constant search after the Unconditional.

---

26. Wariboko, *Pentecostal Principle*, 1.

8

What Is Going On?
The Descriptive Empirical Task

I HAVE PROPOSED WE pay attention to six important characteristics that describe deconstruction. We know deconstruction (1) happens, (2) it happens from the inside, (3) it is not a method, (4) it is call, (5) it is a yes to the other, and (6) it is affirmative of institutions. I have also proposed that there can be a relationship between the work of the Spirit and deconstructive experiences, especially when we take into account these six descriptions from Derrida. In guiding us to all truth, the Spirit also guides us into experiences in which we need to deconstruct certain beliefs to ultimately help us mature our faith in Christ. Here lies the pastoral concern: How can pastors faithfully help people going through deconstructive experiences? How would a faithful and wise pastoral approach look like in such circumstances?

Considering the four Christian responses to postmodern influences posed by Padgett, it must be obvious by now that I do not agree with simply ignoring (the ostrich) or satanizing (the bogeyman) deconstruction. These responses cannot be regarded as a faithful approach from the church, even if they are common. We are left with two possible responses: seeing deconstruction as our "best buddy" or as a critical dialogue partner.[1] There might be a scenario in which deconstruction *can* be one of our best buddies in faith formation, *if* we engage it in critical dialogue. If being a best buddy is too big of a title, perhaps we could at least see it as an aide.

At this point, the role of the pastor as a practical theologian is of upmost importance. Richard Osmer suggests four core tasks of practical theology. These are born from asking key questions in the pastoral context, the resulting answers are helpful guide to navigate the realities of ministry. The four questions are the following:

1. *What is going on?* (Gathering information to identify patterns or episodes)
2. *Why is this going on?* (Explaining the reasons behind certain patterns)
3. *What ought to be going on?* (Determining good practices)
4. *How might we respond?* (Determining strategies)[2]

These questions will guide the final section of this work, while we consider what would be an appropriate pastoral response to deconstruction of faith from a Latin American Pentecostal perspective.

In the previous chapters I have already started responding to the first pastoral question of "what is going on?" In this short chapter I would like to point to the usefulness of describing faith deconstruction as a process; this will provide a mental structure that pastors can use to better serve their churches.

The experience of faith transformation, how it is deconstructed and reconstructed back again, can be described in many ways. Marcus Borg simply describes it as *memories*, what he observed growing up; *conversions*, major changes in his understanding; and *convictions*, the affirmations flowing from those changes. For Borg, these changes manifested themselves as intellectual, political, and

---

1. Padgett, "Christianity and Postmodernity," 129.
2. Osmer, *Practical Theology*, 4.

religious thoughts and practices.³ Alternatively, Father Rohr sees faith transformation as three boxes people move from; these are *order*, in which everything is explained fairly simply; *disorder*, when our ordered universe disappoints us so we assume the postmodern stance of distrust and skepticism about everything and everyone; and *reorder*, where the best of the conservative and liberal positions come together and "radical traditionalists" love their truth and community enough to critique it without overreacting or overdefending.[4] Brian McLaren likewise uses threefold imagery; he talks about the painful and traumatic death of Good Friday in which we witness the collapse of our faith system, the silent and contemplative Saturday, and the beautiful and deep Easter Sunday where we move from organized religion to organizing religion for the common good.[5]

For his part, A. J. Swoboda, after acknowledging the work of Fowler and Peterson on faith development,[6] also proposes a triple framework: *theological construction*, in which uncritical assent causes good and bad beliefs to be accepted; *theological deconstruction*, which happens when we stop thinking our faith works (at this stage it is hard to differentiate the deconstruction of wrong beliefs from the deconstruction of faith all together); and *reconstruction*, a point that not everyone reaches but is a return to the first love that demands courage and intentionality.[7]

Mark Gregory Karris, who is a therapist and pastor, provides a clearer view of the process a person goes through regarding the deconstruction of faith. He presents the whole experience as a

---

3. Borg, *Convictions*, 19.
4. Rohr, *Universal Christ*, 245–46.
5. McLaren, *Great Spiritual Migration*, 13–14.
6. James Fowler proposed seven stages of faith formation: primal-undifferentiated faith, intuitive-projective faith, mythic-literal faith, synthetic-conventional faith, individuative-reflective faith, conjunctive faith, and universalizing faith; see Fowler, *Stages of Faith*. Eugene Peterson's framework is based on the Pentateuch: Genesis, the prenatal word of God; Exodus, the birth and infancy; Leviticus, childhood; Numbers, adolescence; and Deuteronomy, adulthood; see Peterson, *Working the Angles*, 59–61.
7. Swoboda, *After Doubt*, 23–28.

faith journey with "different stations" along the way. This language helps to avoid the idea that people must move from one place to the other in their faith journey or that one place is superior to the other. I will attempt to summarize Karris' findings on each station as best as I can:[8]

1. *Feeling at home*, church and faith provide emotional security with little doubt.

2. *Splinterhood*, when a person experiences increasing tension and great discomfort from holding together two apparently contradictory ideas, also known as cognitive dissonance.

3. *To be or not to be*, the tension grows to the point that a person feels forced to act. If no action is taken, then psychological defense mechanisms such as repression or suppression take place.

4. *Returning home different*, represents the decision of going back to safe places and relationships with little change. The return might happen out of fear of God, losing relationships, hurting loved ones, or even losing oneself.

5. *Disorientation*, some might travel easily through this station, while others display PTSD symptoms. At this point the person has a very different perception of self, God, and/or church. Even when there are feelings of anger, grief, depression, moral confusion, and similar; these can lead to profound growth and transformation.

6. *Angstville*, the predominant emotion here is anger. This sentiment might be intimidating for the person or those around him; nevertheless, it is valid, especially when we reflect on the witness of imprecatory psalms and laments. Also, we must recognize that some systems of theological or ideological oppression demand an angry response. Some people here still identify as Christians, others leave their faith, and others claim to have left God and church but invest an immense amount of energy against the faith because they still have a

---

8. Karris, *Religious Refugees*, 53–74.

strong relationship with it. Karris believes this station is dangerous because doubt and cynicism can become a person's new faith, some people stuck here might need the proper tools to grieve so post-traumatic church syndrome can become post-traumatic growth.

7. *Farewell and goodbye*, some religious refugees find a new home away from Christian tradition and experience a newfound sense of freedom. Even when they still experience anger against some Christian ideologies, this anger is not reactive but elicits compassionate responses.

8. *Extreme Makeover-Home Edition*, at this station we find those believers who have embraced profound growth and transformation. They have fused fundamentalist and progressive faith, and they belief in a God who is greater than any human understanding but are still on a life-long search. Instead of control, they long for intimacy. They embrace paradox and mystery. They love the church as a living organism.

This helpful work shows that the three-step paradigm commonly used in books that address the subject of deconstruction of faith is an oversimplification of a very complex reality. Even when virtually every author acknowledges it is a process that may take years, the three-step paradigm may still give the idea that things will sort themselves out in a matter of months. Karris's contribution provides further insight on the emotional and social aspects experienced during the faith journey when he identifies five symptoms of what he calls religious disorientation growth syndrome:[9]

1. Doubting or denying beliefs once held to be true.
2. Anxiety about one's relationship with God.
3. Increase of painful emotions.
4. Feared or realized isolation and criticism from family members or faith community.
5. Existential angst about one's identity and future.

9. Karris, *Religious Refugees*, 18–19.

It is clear that a person may need the support of a therapist in some parts of his or her faith journey; the different experiences identified by the author cannot be solved solely by counseling, teaching, or prayer. It is also important for pastors to understand that sometimes a third party can provide a safe place to process all things related to this journey; after all, a person may be questioning even the pastor's role, authority, or good intentions. Wise pastors connect people to multiple resources because they understand they cannot, and should not, do it all.

Conclusion, the Descriptive-Empirical Task

Pastors do not engage in the descriptive-empirical task out of mere curiosity about what is going on. The pastoral heart longs to answer this question because it practices a spirituality of presence: "[The] spiritual orientation of attending to others in their particularity and otherness . . . with openness, attentiveness, and prayerfulness."[10] Being present in this way is what allows pastors to be faithful to Christ, their calling, and church; the concept of a spirituality of presence describes the kind of pastor that people going through deconstructive experiences need.

---

10. Osmer, *Practical Theology*, 34.

9

Why Is This Going On?
The Interpretive Task

THE INTERPRETIVE TASK SEEKS to answer the question *why is this going on?* There are multiple reasons that might lead a person to deconstruct her faith. It would be a mistake to try to identify the reason why someone deconstructs her faith just so we can judge whether we consider that experience to be valid or not, in the end regardless of the reason a pastor still needs to address the final result and being judgmental about a person's experience will not help the process. The real value of comprehending why something happens in the life of someone is that it may allow us to better empathize with the person while helping her navigate through important, life-changing experiences.

I would like to submit a few possible causes for consideration, while this list is far from being exhaustive it reflects some of the most common reasons for deconstruction of faith that I have ran into.

Differentiation

For some people, deconstruction is a natural part of their development and maturity; it is a way of finding and asserting one's identity in contrast to that of parents or other significant people in one's life.[1] Healthy development requires "individuals [to] wrestle with issues of identity, meaning, beliefs, goals and their own behavior . . . [so they can] gain a clearer sense of self in relationship with those around them. . . . Where the *I* stops and the *Thou* begins."[2]

This need for differentiation may lead someone to explore different churches, traditions, or relational circles or even to leave faith for a season (sometimes forever). Many times, the spiritual formation received in previous stages of life will prove insufficient for current life experiences, especially if discipleship was conceived as a mere class or course. Both factors, the need for leaving a church, tradition, or faith, and finding previous spiritual formation was insufficient, reminds pastors of the importance of a discipleship process approached from a lifelong perspective, discipleship is learning by walking together. When discipleship is practiced in this way it takes the form of a meaningful relationship. This allows mentoring to happen even if two people no longer share the same faith; but never forget, discipleship is more than mentoring someone, it is missionally oriented, a calling to repent, surrender, and follow Christ.

Intellectual or Theological Curiosity

For others, deconstruction may start as a sincere search for truth and beauty,[3] two things usually obscured in rigid religious contexts. A local church's inability or unwillingness to approach certain subjects forces the person to find answers outside of his faith tradition. Many people turn to their own churches and pastors first when trying to figure out genuine questions and doubts, only to end up disappointed by dismissive attitudes because ministers feel threatened or insecure when confronted to these questions. People in this age have easy access to the rich and varied history of Christian interpretation. This is not a menace and churchgoers

---

1. See Swoboda, *After Doubt*, 10.
2. Balswick et al., *Reciprocating Self*, 202.
3. Zahnd, *When Everything is On Fire*, 49.

Why Is This Going On?

are not sinning when they are trying to deepen their faith; pastors must rise to the occasion and put effort in learning how to navigate these questions with wisdom.

Even when it is tempting to try to fit Christian doctrine into the modern ideal of certainty and predictability, we must understand that theology is not made up of mathematical formulas; this may be hard to understand for people, either pastors or churchgoers, who have been discipled by a modern worldview. Addressing deep and meaningful questions is a challenge that can make even the most experienced pastor tremble; but I can assure you that theological shallowness and anti-intellectualism are not the way. These are harmful and should be eradicated from the local church.

Cultural Shock

Christian faith does not oppose or condemn everything a culture has to offer. Miroslav Volf observes that "Christian identity in a culture is always a complex and flexible network of small and large refusals, divergences, subversions, and more or less radical and encompassing alternative proposals and enactments, surrounded by the acceptance of many cultural givens. There is no single way to relate to a given culture."[4] Christian faith recognizes that whatever humans *value* many times reflects what they *worship*. If the church were to agree with everything valued by its surrounding culture it would cease to be salt and light; as Um and Buzzard say, "if a ministry in the city is not contextualized to challenge a city's unique idolatry, then our ministry will be shallow and unsubstantial."[5]

When faced with certain moral decisions some believers might start having "a perception that Christianity is significantly out of touch with contemporary values."[6] This may be a shocking

---

4. Volf, *Public Faith*, 93.

5. Um and Buzzard, *Why Cities Matter*, 113.

6. McGrath is referring explicitly to the subject of heresy, it is important to clarify that deconstruction does not necessarily lead to it; nevertheless, his insight is still valuable for the subject of deconstruction in general. McGrath, *Heresy*, 180.

experience that leads them to search for moral answers elsewhere. I think this is part of the urgency that led Volf and Croasmun to state that "the purpose of theology is to discern, articulate, and commend visions of flourishing life in light of God's self-revelation in Jesus Christ.... [Then] the core of our response toward moral decline—where and when it exists—should be to articulate a *positive* vision life that calls us *forward*."[7] The pastor's vocation demands she elucidates such visions of a flourishing life compellingly enough to call the congregation to live forward, towards worshiping and valuing something better.

Toxic Environments

Scot McKnight and Laura Barringer warn about *narcissistic leadership* and *power imposed by fear* being the early signs of toxic cultures in churches.[8] Toxic leaders thrive in environments of imposition, shame, and manipulation. While toxic leaders *demonize* questioning, it must be clarified that just because a leader does not know how to handle questioning does not mean he or she is toxic; it may just be a matter of personal development at an intellectual or emotional level. Toxic environments are hotbeds for spiritual abuse and trauma.

Positions of authority in religious organizations carry inherent power. From this standpoint Diane Langberg clarifies the concept of spiritual abuse: "When we use God's sacred Word in a way that harms another, commanding them to do wrong, manipulating them, deceiving them, or humiliating them, we have spiritually abused them.... [Even more] one cannot sexually, physically, or verbally abuse another person without also inflicting spiritual abuse."[9] Her assertion cannot be stressed enough—any and every form of abuse inflicts spiritual abuse. We are whole beings that cannot be compartmentalized; perhaps we instinctively have this notion since a person

---

7. Volf and Croasmun, *For the Life*, 11, 53.
8. See chapter 3 of McKnight and Barringer, *Church Called Tov.*
9. Langberg, *Redeeming Power*, 127.

who has suffered abuse finds it very hard to separate the abuser's deeds from the abuser's faith. Once a person is aware of the toxicity present in a church's environment, it is only natural that they would start questioning or simply rejecting everything related to it, even the legitimate parts of Christianity that were used to manipulate the person into illegitimate behaviors and beliefs.

Disappointment and Pain

Disappointment and pain can be strong forces that define a person's journey with God in the midst of disorienting experiences. Enns addresses this reality: "Life happens, and when it does, it wreaks havoc with our neatly arranged thoughts of God, the world, and our place in it . . . until 'certainty' becomes past tense."[10] Multiple reasons can trigger these feelings: innocent misunderstandings within the congregation, political stances of leadership, personal sickness, or the heartbreaking pain of loss.

Sometimes disappointment produced by human failure or life experiences causes a disconnect from spiritually nurturing relationships that lead people to cut ties with the church, friends, or mentors. This can lead to a neglected faith that gradually extinguishes because communal life is foundational for a healthy Christian faith. Self-isolation, regardless of the reason, can inadvertently numb the heart.

Avoiding pain and stretching towards happiness is only human, this urge is not bad or sinful, but also is not always possible. When we run into unavoidable suffering, we naturally turn to our theological beliefs hoping these can spare us. Enns describes the experience of suffering as "the place where our sense of certainty about God's ways fades like a dream and forces us to consider that what we know may not be as central to our faith as we might think"; a reconfiguration of our deepest beliefs takes place when we walk through suffering.[11] At this point, pain might seem to be

---

10. Enns, *Sin of Certainty*, 118.
11. Enns, *Sin of Certainty*, 134.

catastrophic to faith, but Gulley's voice gives us hope: "Consider this great irony: the very pain and suffering we'd hoped to avoid by becoming religious is often the very means by which our spiritual wholeness, integrity, and happiness become possible."[12] First Peter 1:6–7 reminds us that faith is not fragile, even if it feels that way sometimes; our faith is actually refined through the fires of life.

The biblical witness shows with transparency that deep reconfiguration of faith was needed in the face of multiple faith-shattering events like the Babylonian exile or Job's experience. Pastors should incorporate into their pastoral toolbox the wisdom found in the imprecatory Psalms, Job, Lamentations, and other similar writings that address the vulnerability of the human soul and avoid promising a quasi-magical faith that makes life virtually free of trials. Believing in miracles, as Pentecostals do, does not entail denying reality or making false promises. The wisdom literature found in the Hebrew Bible is not just intended for theoretical teachings, but for real, pastoral ministry that deals with the crudeness of life. The kind of loving heart needed in such instances is very well described by Gulley: "They did for us what loving people should do—they tenderly assisted us when we were crippled, then empowered us to stand and walk again."[13]

Discipleship

Even when this may be the least cited reason for deconstruction, I believe the right discipleship process helps a person navigate through deconstruction. Mentors should heed the different causes of deconstruction and stand by the disciple's side in order to assist him or her.

Furthermore, I think we should envision a discipleship process that *leads* a person to deconstruct his or her faith *within the local church*, challenging the disciple's beliefs and leading them into deep questioning of their assumptions, connecting them

---

12. Gulley, *Evolution of Faith*, 115.
13. Gulley, *Evolution of Faith*, 121.

Why Is This Going On?

to different resources, voices, and perspectives that enrich their worldview and teaching them how to deal with these. Book clubs, interfaith *dialogue* (not evangelism), missional projects, communal service, development of theological imagination, teaching them how loving the neighbor looks in practice . . . these are just some examples of experiences that can help produce disciples that are better suited to face the current context; disciples that not only read the Bible, but actually understand how to apply its truth to their lives. The faith community should be a place of dialogue and wonder; in other words, Christlike discipleship.

Conclusion, the Interpretive Task

I would like to highlight that the only one of the aforementioned reasons for deconstruction that is malignant by itself is *toxic environments*; its malevolence does not spring from a person's response to it but from the evil it incubates. In this case, deconstruction may literally save a person's life. All the other reasons might be instruments used by the Spirit to bring a person to maturity and a deeper relationship with God, especially when accompanied by faithful pastoral ministry.

Osmer shows that the reason pastors care about the interpretive task is because they understand that *wise judgment*, the practical wisdom needed at the local church, comes from the marriage between *thoughtfulness* that considers how a person experiences something, and *theoretical interpretation* of knowledge from the sciences and the arts.[14]

Theoretical interpretation plays a key role in helping pastors deal with deconstructive experiences, but it is not enough to act wisely. Each cause for deconstruction requires a thoughtful pastoral heart that is aware of both the emotions related to these experiences and the time it takes for people to journey through processes like these. What Borg calls conversion events may be "sudden and

---

14. Osmer, *Practical Theology*, 82–84.

dramatic . . . or, more commonly, gradual and accumulative";[15] the rate at which these changes happen is usually related to the causes that produced them in the first place. Pastors know that caring for the flock is a lifelong commitment that yields results over years, not days or months. It is tempting for Pentecostals to expect miraculous short-term results, but we must remember that the work of God on the disciples extended long before and after Pentecost. Pastors know that sometimes the greatest miracles take time.

---

15. Borg, *Convictions*, 28.

10

What Ought to Be Going On?

The Normative Task

To engage in the normative task and define what ought to be going on, it will be helpful to have a broader vision of pastoral theology. Pastoral theology is by nature practical with a keen interest in pastoral care: "The art of pastoral theology explores the rationale, nature and ethos of care, as practiced by and through communities of faith. Pastoral theology, which is by its very nature a reflective practice, can be found in the various caring activities of persons and communities."[1] This particular strand of theology is concerned with the divine-human relationship; it is rooted and tested in practice, and it arises from specific historical, geographical, sociopolitical, economic, and cultural contexts.[2] According to Woodward and Pattison, pastoral theology is transformational because it works towards making a difference not only in a person's understanding but in his or her actual life situation. It addresses the human situation holistically, bringing together logical propositions, human emotions, the *symbolic*, and even what may appear as irrational, making the religious experience relevant in a person's life. Pastoral theology proudly embraces the adjective of

1. Lartey, *Pastoral Theology*, 3.
2. Lartey, *Pastoral Theology*, 5, 12.

unsystematic, in Woodward and Pattison's view, since it makes no claim to universal validity because of its highly contextual nature.³

The Cambridge Dictionary of Christian Theology explains four main models of pastoral theology:⁴

1. The **classical-clerical** is characterized by its emphasis on the office, role, and functions of clergy as ministers of the *cura animarum* (the cure of souls).

2. The **clinical-pastoral** sees the pastor as a trained clinician and understands pastoral care as mental health.

3. The **communal-contextual** gives preference to the community over the individual, it sees care as communitarian in nature and understands personal distress as interconnected with sociopolitical conditions, which is why it is heavily influenced by contextual theologies such as liberation, feminist, and black theologies.

4. The **intercultural-postmodern** model uses sociocultural analysis to deliver pastoral care, incorporating theological anthropology that celebrates differences such as gender, race, class, culture, and sexuality as opportunities for honest dialogue.

Carrie Doehring finds the classical-clerical paradigm to be insufficient; in her opinion its focus on "the authority of the Bible, personal commitment to Jesus, and belief in fundamental creedal statements"⁵ might lead pastors to prioritize right beliefs, as generic principles, over well-being. She also warns pastors to be wary of focusing on individual healing (probably referring to the clinical-pastoral paradigm), which is appealing because of its resonance with "modern middle-class Euro-American values: personal autonomy, individual freedom, and a belief in progress, along with a non-moralistic use of religion that focuses on self-actualization

---

3. Woodward and Pattison, *Blackwell Reader*, 13–16.
4. Lartey, "Pastoral Theology," 372.
5. Doehring, *Practice of Pastoral Care*, xx.

What Ought to Be Going On?

and personal growth."[6] Doehring prefers contextual and postmodern models of pastoral care that set context-specific goals; for example, *sustaining* by offering communal care in contexts that do not allow the person's healing to be fully realized (proposed by African American pastoral theologians), or *survival* (suggested by feminist pastoral theologians). Willimon sees the ancient *cura animarum* of the classical-clerical paradigm as a critique of secular therapy whose goal is self-fulfillment: "The gospel is a critique of our needs, an attempt to give us needs worth having."[7] From the same standpoint, he understands pastoral care as communal edification that is highly contextualized because it takes place in the community of believers. Perhaps the four main models of pastoral theology are not necessarily exclusive since they approach the pastoral task from different perspectives and propose tools that can complement each other. But of course, the focus one chooses will shape the pastoral work with a person and a community.

The pastor should be mindful of the heavy Western influences found in the classical-clerical and clinical-pastoral models. On the other hand, it would be naive to assume the communal-contextual and intercultural-postmodern are unpolluted from other influences; we have already learned there is no such thing as an objective approach. The value found in these last two models is the focus on location that helps pastors better address specific needs in the community of faith. Now, if other Christian communities around the world have found value in any of these four models, pastors should be open to learn with a critical mind and to contribute with their own findings from the local context.

Doehring suggests the work of pastoral care theologians should differentiate between *life-giving* and *life-limiting* beliefs, values, and coping mechanisms. Contextual goals in pastoral ministry should embody compassion that addresses life-limiting theologies of fear and shame and is sustained by personal and communal spiritual practices.[8] A pastor who is walking with a

---

6. Doehring, *Practice of Pastoral Care*, xix.
7. Willimon, *Pastor*, 95–96.
8. Doehring, *Practice of Pastoral Care*, xx.

believer through a deconstruction process will find herself helping them distinguish between these life-giving and life-limiting beliefs. Doehring suggests the use of Pargament's spiritual orienting systems[9] to help us define what is life-giving or not; the following criteria should be met:

1. **Differentiation of Meaning-Making.** Are religious and theological beliefs owned by the person? Can they fully articulate them? Do these beliefs help the person transform distress into "empathic concern and compassion where love propels care seekers to reach out rather than withdraw"?[10]

2. **Integration and Flexibility.** Refers to the integration of spiritual practices that produce love, joy, contentment, and similar emotions. Integrating these practices and emotions to daily life should provide flexibility that makes a difference in how the person deals with moments of suffering, fear and similar emotions. Fragmentation and inflexibility show life-limiting beliefs.[11]

3. **Beliefs and Spiritual Practices Related to Benevolence and Goodness.** The last criterion explores if a person's spiritual practices help her experience the goodness of God as respect, trust, and compassion with themselves, others, and God. A life-giving theology is a lived theology that connects people with the goodness of God through different means.[12]

These orienting systems serve as healthy guidelines that can shape the pastoral work with a person who is facing deconstructive experiences.

Now I would like to take a few more steps towards a pastoral theology that celebrates the Pentecostal identity.

---

9. See Pargament et al., "Spirituality: A Pathway."
10. Doehring, *Practice of Pastoral Care*, 91.
11. Doehring, *Practice of Pastoral Care*, 92.
12. Doehring, *Practice of Pastoral Care*, 93.

What Ought to Be Going On?

A Pentecostal Pastoral Theology

The pastoral work as presented by Doehring is to be done by using what she calls a trifocal lens that considers a *precritical focus* that understands that the sacred can be glimpsed, apprehended, and expressed through sacred texts; a *modern focus* that reflects on rational and empirical methods like critical interpretation and social sciences; and a *postmodern focus* which understands the contextual and provisional nature of knowledge, even knowledge about God.[13] A skilled pastor should learn to move between the different focal points and find ways in which each one complements the others. The balance between sensibility and critical thinking found in Doehring's trifocal lens can make a great difference when pastoring Pentecostal believers.

Castelo and Castelo show the importance of a similar methodology when they address the subject of how to care for the mystical soul of a Pentecostal:

> The mystical sensibilities within Pentecostalism are precious and worth lifting up; however, they are also precarious and so require intentional care and stewardship. . . . The mystical sensibilities of Pentecostalism thrive when things are running smoothly and people claim deliverance, see miracles happen, and generally feel like God is at work and doing something on their behalf. However, when things break down, when people are bound in cycles of sin and self-destruction, and when miracles do not happen despite the steady prayers of the faithful over years of tarrying, what then? Pentecostals at such points have a much harder time living into their spirituality with confidence and, as a result, may significantly struggle. Some may even leave the Christian faith altogether.[14]

Three recommendations are to be considered when caring for Pentecostals. First, "that the intimate relationship between the mystic and God ought to be affirmed throughout the process of

---

13. Doehring, *Practice of Pastoral Care*, xxv.
14. Castelo and Castelo, "Caring for Contemporary Mystics," 109.

care. For the mystic, God represents . . . a 'safe haven.' . . . Western contexts tend to pathologize dependency, whereas attachment theory sees it as complementary to autonomy."[15] The security found in God orients a person towards vulnerability, honesty, and acceptance, thereby making them resilient people. Second, the pastor must work out of the apophatic conviction "that the Spirit is constantly at work, whether the carer or the cared see it or not."[16] And third, by realizing that "caring for contemporary mystics involves stepping into another kind of world,"[17] the pastor or caretaker will deal with mystic souls in careful and generous manners.

From a Pentecostal perspective I would say the emphasis the classical-clerical paradigm places on the office of the pastor risks losing sight of the pneumatic community in which every single believer has been filled with the Spirit to minister to one another. I am not saying that every person should lead counseling sessions or minister through personal prayer to a person in need of pastoral care, there are plenty of stories that exemplify how the mix of good intentions and poor preparation causes more damage than good. Still, we should conceive the Pentecostal local church as a community of healing or more exactly a community of discipleship in which healing is always available. This is a place in which the body can and should minister to one another according to their gifts. Here the role of the pastor is essential in orchestrating the healing community, connecting people to different resources, introducing them to the right people, creating opportunities for mutual service and learning. The concept of a healing community also reminds us that healthy pastors never isolate people, they always connect them to life-giving relationships.

On the other hand, Pentecostals must recognize the strength that the classical-clerical paradigm provides because of its connection to centuries of rich reflection on the pastoral ministry. The Latin American Pentecostal tradition downplays its connection to historical Christianity out of anti-Catholic sentiments, effectively

---

15. Castelo and Castelo, "Caring for Contemporary Mystics," 110.
16. Castelo and Castelo, "Caring for Contemporary Mystics," 112.
17. Castelo and Castelo, "Caring for Contemporary Mystics," 114.

depriving itself from a wealth of resources and deep reflection on the pastoral ministry. Any model in which the Spirit is placed at the center can be life-giving; the pastor should constantly ask relevant questions amid the Spirit's movement in the congregation and its immediate context. That is why pastoral theology should not only consider the classical-clerical paradigm, but also the clinical, contextual, and postmodern dimensions of ministry. In doing so, the whole community of faith is invited to follow the Spirit in very specific ways; otherwise, we threaten pneumatic creativity by replacing dependance on the Holy Spirit with recipe-like answers (e.g., "pray more," "take this course," "do this test").

For Pentecostals, the pastor does not minister to the community from above but from within. The pastor is one anointed believer among many anointed believers, called to serve his or her community with a specific authority that is exercised lovingly for the sake of an empowered people. Wilkins succinctly points out some of the main differences in how different faith traditions approach pastoral theology.[18] According to him, the Roman Catholic emphasis on sin as the problem produces a pastoral theology concerned with the nurture of souls and their preparation for heaven. The Lutheran emphasis on faithlessness (pride, self-righteousness, lack of trust, and anxiety) yields a pastoral theology preoccupied with inducing feelings of despair and repentance, followed by encouragement to have faith. Anglican pastoral theology seeks to restore order by embodying the grace of God because of its conception of sin as an inward, interpersonal, and social disorder. Reformed pastoral theology is concerned with the Christian need for concrete assurance of their foreordination to salvation, leading to a focus on procedures to determine the true state of souls and achieving evidence of their security.

A Pentecostal approach to pastoral theology would gravitate around its self-understanding as a renewal movement, remaining radically open to the unexpected move of Spirit, while connecting the individual to a charismatic community by an emotive, narrative epistemology. To be clearer, the resulting pastoral theology would

---

18. Wilkins, "Pastoral Theology," 876.

help believers locate themselves within the story of God and the people of God, allowing the Spirit to guide them into new seasons of renewal and growth within the divine purposes. The sensibility of being a movement and the value of participation would bring the pastor and the believer into a relationship of equals in which the pastor understands herself as being in a position of authority expressed as a gift to the believer. The relationship would have the mark of *koinonia*, following the trinitarian example. Furthermore, the Pentecostal minister follows the pattern set by the *paraklētos* (John 14:16, 26; 15:26; 16:7; Acts 9:31), understanding oneself as called to the ministry of *paraklēsis* (Acts 13:15; 15:31; Rom 12:8; 1 Cor 14:3), coming alongside to encourage, comfort, and console the people of God which can be achieved either by verbal or nonverbal means.[19] The holistic nature of a Pentecostal pastoral theology would result in a genuine concern for the full well-being of the believer, validating emotional responses and allowing them to find expression in the presence of God and the community.

Conclusion, the Normative Task

The goal of bringing all these factors together is to help Latin American Pentecostal pastors engage in the pastoral normative task by *prophetically discerning good pastoral practices* that foster not only life-giving theologies, but life-giving deconstructive processes. Osmer points out that "prophetic discernment is the task of listening to this Word and interpreting it in ways that address particular social conditions, events, and decisions before congregations today."[20] Prophetic discernment is particular not only in its time and place, but also regarding the person ministered by it.

This particularity takes place thanks to a very important factor in prophetic discernment as presented by Osmer: sympathy. Sympathy is the participation in God's pathos, his suffering over

---

19. According to Louw and Nida, *Greek-English Lexicon*.
20. Osmer, *Practical Theology*, 135.

What Ought to Be Going On?

the life experiences of his people.[21] We are reminded of the importance of this identification in suffering by the use the rabbis gave to the term *Shekinah*. This word is used to describe the presence of God that so identifies with his people that when they go into exile so does God's presence. When they come back, *Shekinah* once again comes back with them; "what the Lord does to Israel he does to himself, in that the Shekinah shares Israel's *lot* and the Lord's *being*."[22] Such identification is echoed by God's ministers, the prophets; Hebrew Bible scholar Ellen Davis points out "Israelite prophets ... characteristically suffered *along with* the people— their own people."[23] The prophetic ministry of discernment in pastoral work should never be divorced of the Pentecostal conception of ministering from within, not from above; this does not mean necessarily sharing the same experience as the person, but sympathetically coming along their side in the spirit of *paraklēsis*.

But in order for prophetic discernment to be transformed into good practices (normativity), sympathy is not enough, it must be met with theological and ethical interpretation.[24] Theological interpretation refers to the pastoral work of struggling with theological concepts so particular situations can be interpreted in light of Christian tradition and biblical truth. Ethical reflection happens when principles, rules, or guidelines are used to arrive to moral actions. Richard B. Hays proposes an approach to Christian ethics that grants authority to the biblical text of the New Testament in the mode in which it speaks: "[We must] respect not only its content [the New Testament's] but also its form. . . . The Christian tradition witnesses to the importance of the New Testament's claim in all four of the modes that we have delineated: rule, principle, paradigm and symbolic world."[25] A rule refers to straightforward instructions such as "do not lie to each other" (Col 3:9 NIV). A principle would be our attitude toward work because

---

21. Osmer, *Practical Theology*, 136.
22. Jenson, *Systematic Theology*, 76.
23. Davis, *Biblical Prophecy*, 101. As testified in Jas 5:10.
24. Osmer, *Practical Theology*, 136, 161.
25. Hays, *Moral Vision of the New Testament*, 294.

Deconstruction and the Spirit

we understand all we do is for the Lord (Col 3:23). Paradigms are exemplary persons we are called to imitate for example Mary and her devotion to God in heart, soul, and body, or Zacchaeus's reaction to the gospel as opposed to the rich young ruler. The symbolic world refers to how do we live in light of the biblical idea of God as the Creator and giver of live or how we treat fellow human beings if we understand they are bearers of God's image. Hays makes these distinctions not only because he finds them in the biblical text, but because many interpreters tend to reduce the scriptural approach to ethics to one single mode, overriding biblical truth that is expressed through different manners. Each mode can be approached with different levels of literality and creativity while maintaining their authority and all should be taken into account to enrich our understanding.

When it comes to developing good practices, Andrew Root makes a valid warning to pastors living in a secular age about how tempting it is "[to] ask for a program, a bullet-pointed to-do list, a new model, or a direct script for how to operationalize this reality in your church. . . . Wanting the pragmatic—that works!—over encounters with divine being itself."[26] It is very easy to fall into this temptation in order to avoid the anxiety of not knowing exactly what to do, but not knowing what to do is not only part of being a pastor, is part of living through faith. Mystery plays a big role in what pastors do. Eugene Peterson closes his book *The Pastor* with a letter to a young minister that reminds us of the ambiguity ever-present in ministry:

> Being a pastor is unique across the spectrum of vocations. Not better, not privileged, not anything special, but unique in society as a whole. . . . It amazes me still how much of the time I simply don't know what I am doing, don't know what to say, don't know what the next move is. . . . Unfortunately, there are many "ways of escape" in which we can exercise and develop areas of administrative or therapeutic or scholarly or programmatic

---

26. Root, *Pastor in a Secular Age*, 272.

competences in the church and in doing so avoid the ambiguity of being a pastor.[27]

We should be careful not to use resources and knowledge as way to escape spending time with God in the midst of mystery, but good practices are developed through the exploration of models of good practice present and past. Pastors should not only weight them wisely, but feel free to experiment wisely, carefully trying new approaches and assessing their impact in the congregation. Dismissing models or programs just because they are models or programs is not wise, but I do believe pastors should break free of the modern ideal of being objective observers, with proven universal strategies that provide straightforward answers to every and any problem. We pastors work out of the conviction that we have been called for a purpose within our congregations; let God be God while we strive to be faithful.

---

27. Peterson, *Pastor*, 315.

11

How Might We Respond?
The Pragmatic Task

I HAVE RESPONDED TO the following questions: "What is going on? Why is this going on? And, what ought to be going on?" (The descriptive, the interpretive, and the normative tasks.) I will now attempt to address the pragmatic task: "How might we respond?" First, we must go back to the ancient prophecy found in Isaiah and the first letter written by the apostle Paul to the church in Corinth. I believe the input received by these sources will allow us to draw out a pastoral approach to communities going through deconstructive processes.

The Promise for the Community in Isaiah

As we saw earlier, Caputo traces back Derrida's term *déconstruction* to the prophet Isaiah's declaration: "So once again I will do things that shock and amaze them, and I will destroy the wisdom of those who claim to know and understand" (Isa 29:14 CEV). God is warning his people that he is about to tear down the thought structures that give them confidence, because these are unable to provide the assurance they attribute to them. In their dullness they

How Might We Respond?

are missing "the wonderful and marvelous actions of God."[1] So the Lord is about to destroy and renew their faith. This *divine destruction* has affinities to the idea we now know as deconstruction of faith.

Seitz points out that "the shapers of the Isaiah traditions have worked with the overwhelming conviction that God's word to Israel in the past was uttered to instruct the present and future generations."[2] We can conclude that at some point, someone constructed something over the word uttered by God that needed to be destroyed and made new for the people of God to enjoy the benefits of God's promises.

The Lord's everlasting faithfulness leads him to provide for his people whatever is necessary to help them face the challenge of the destruction and renewal of their faith. To them, God promises the care of a shepherd: "The Lord cares for his nation, just as shepherds care for their flocks. He carries the lambs in his arms, while gently leading the mother sheep" (Isa 40:11 CEV). Even when the book is a "collage" of different messages for different occasions, it was arranged as one book; as such, "there is something to learn from the total arrangement."[3] This means that even when the challenge and the promise are in different sections, the fact that tradition has treated it as one coherent message allows us to find a relationship between God's challenge and his promise to his people.

According to John Goldingay, one of the main problems the Isaiah community faced was that their leaders made alliances with death by sincerely treating false promises as certain refuges. They claimed to be devoted, but their strategies did not include God. The sincerity of their mistakes did not free them from the consequences of hurting the people of God, because they lived as if they wanted the voice of YHWH to be silenced.[4] This is the reason God himself caused the destruction of their wisdom so that the divine wisdom could be manifested.

1. Seitz, *Isaiah 1–39*, 215.
2. Seitz, *Isaiah 1–39*, 18.
3. Goldingay, *Theology of the Book*, 11–12.
4. Goldingay, *Theology of the Book*, 54–55.

Deconstruction and the Spirit

In the language of the Hebrew Bible, leaders were referred to as shepherds. In this context sheep could be lost either by being abandoned or by wandering away. When we address the topic of deconstruction of faith, it is usually assumed that the sheep are wandering away, which of course could be the case: people often deconstruct their way out of faith in Christ. But one should never forget that the problem that the sheep in Isaiah faced involved *abandonment by their leaders*.[5] In the context of deconstructive experiences, pastors abandon their congregation when they dismiss their doubts, ignore the negative effects of certain theologies, fail to walk beside them in difficult seasons, or even when they preach defensively, aggressively, or lightly.

The Isaiah community lost "nearly all of those structures and institutions which [gave] identity to community."[6] This threw them into a pit of hopelessness and despair where questioning God's goodness and love was a logical reaction. It is in this context in which the powerful image of the shepherd is introduced to reassure God's people that their protector and sustainer was still present.[7] In fact, such is the power of this promise that this passage was incorporated by the ancient church as an Advent lection, showing a God who enters "into the confusion of human affairs."[8] A deconstructing people needs a present shepherd who enters into the confusion surrounding the congregation to care, sometimes even carry, and always gently leading.

From the Christian perspective, the motif of Messiah as shepherd is most fully developed in the Gospel of John where the Good Shepherd is contrasted to a thief or a stranger. Here the shepherd "is the means by which God blesses and protects his people."[9] Gerard Sloyan underlines the Christological importance of this passage in showing "the unparalleled intimacy between Jesus and the Father

---

5. Johnson, "Shepherd, Sheep," 751.
6. Hanson, *Isaiah 40–66*, 14.
7. Hanson, *Isaiah 40–66*, 24–25.
8. Hanson, *Isaiah 40–66*, 32.
9. Johnson, "Shepherd, Sheep," 752.

How Might We Respond?

and the effect of his laying down his life freely for his sheep."[10] The text clearly makes claims that cannot be made of any other shepherd but Christ, especially when one realizes the political overtones of the text, which stretch further than our modern ideas of pastoral care. In Sloyan's view the use of the word καλός (*kalos*)[11] points to Jesus' role as "the human repository of all the powers and functions of Israel's Lord."[12] He also warns about the dangers of pastors who might "identify themselves with the 'noble shepherd' at all points,"[13] a temptation that has led preachers in the past to lightly assume the position of a good shepherd while conveniently placing their "opponents" in the position of thieves and robbers.

This warning reminds us to fight the temptation of finding a human equivalent for all of the Good Shepherd's characteristics. Nevertheless, before the Gospel of John is finished, in chapter 21, the metaphor of the shepherd is applied *to* the disciples *by* Jesus himself, pointing us to believe that the Good Shepherd has discipled good shepherds to carry on his work.[14] In fact, others think that the use of καλός instead of the alternative ἀγαθός (*agathos*), a word that describes something supremely righteous, points to the divine invitation to imitate Christ.[15]

One needs to heed Sloyan's warning without omitting the fact that the teaching of the Good Shepherd originates from a controversy between Jesus and the Pharisees; it is in this context in which Jesus contrasts a good shepherd against "thieves and wolves." When Paul uses the image of a shepherd to refer to church leadership, he also warns about the presence of vicious wolves who are people who pervert the truth, do not spare the flock, and draw disciples away (Acts 20:28–31). The same shepherd metaphor to is used in 1 Peter to refer to the elders of the church while also mentioning a roaring lion who brings suffering (1 Pet 5:1–11).

10. Sloyan, *John*, 139.
11. Not only beautiful and delightful, but noble.
12. Sloyan, *John*, 128.
13. Sloyan, *John*, 130.
14. Johnson, "Shepherd, Sheep," 753.
15. Gunter, "For the Flock," 10–11.

Gunther recognizes several characteristics attributed to the Good Shepherd throughout John's Gospel, but he finds the emphasis from a pastoral point of view is in the shepherd's heart motivation, more than his leadership tactics.[16] As pastors, we crave for the safety of tactics, but these do not necessarily apply in different contexts. *A pastoral heart, on the other hand, is always required and will work in any context, faithfully striving to find tactics for the specific reality of the local church.*

A pastoral heart is of upmost relevance when encountering the challenges presented by deconstruction of faith. Some of these challenges have to do with diversity in beliefs, the relational aspect of faith, and finding a purpose behind divine destruction and renewal of faith.

The Challenge of Diversity in Beliefs

One of the challenges pastors deal with is the broad range of beliefs a person can have, even amongst Christian faith. The most extreme deviations from Christian faith are called heresies. In fact, Rhyne R. Putman wisely emphasizes such a term does not apply to "every interpretive mistake or error."[17] He considers the label "heresy" only applies to those beliefs or teachings that amount to the abandonment of faith. McGrath finds that heresy formulates core Christian beliefs in ways that can be not only inadequate, but even destructive; nevertheless, he believes there "lies a penumbra of views"[18] between orthodoxy and heresy. Some evangelical thinkers are quick to brand as heresy any form of deconstruction, but many times they fail to consider that, more than there being a penumbra of views between both extremes, orthodoxy itself is quite generous and more diverse than many seem to recognize.

Even if we consider a belief as heretical, McGrath finds "no real grounds for supposing that heresy was the outcome of malevolent

---

16. Gunter, "For the Flock," 9.
17. Putman, *When Doctrine Divides*, 206.
18. McGrath, *Heresy*, 12.

How Might We Respond?

and arrogant apostates plotting to destroy Christianity,"[19] despite what some early Christian writers asserted and what many anti-deconstructionists allege today. Even if a belief is found to be destructive, this does not mean the person proposing it has malevolent intentions. Such distinction directly impacts how a pastor addresses a situation.

A pastoral heart is aware of the existence of false teachers, inside and outside the church. However, pastors remember that not every differing idea or question is ill-intended. A pastoral heart is open to dialogue and even to some level of challenge, always assuming people have honest intentions until proven otherwise. Pastors know they can be wrong and understand there is plenty of room in orthodoxy for differing opinions, which is why they are committed to continuous personal growth that allows them to identify generous theological areas, as well as unnegotiable arenas. Ministry teams will also prove helpful for pastors to welcome a diversity of opinions to enrich their work.

Putman clarifies that doctrinal disagreements come from different sources: we read imperfectly, we read differently, we reason differently, we feel differently, and we have different biases. He suggests that when we come in contact with divergent readings we should start first by assessing if there really is a disagreement at all and not a simple matter of differing semantics. For Putman, sometimes we just use different concepts to portray the same idea (e.g., Nicaea's metaphysics differ from Paul's language but attempt to portray the same concepts), or read the same text within different contexts.[20] If we find there is an actual disagreement, we must approach it with epistemic virtue: "Curiosity, intellectual honesty, teachability, patience, discernment, creativity, and wisdom."[21] Then we should consider who is in a better interpretive position; this refers to a person's studies and knowledge on the matter. If we

---

19. McGrath, *Heresy*, 175.

20. Putman, *When Doctrine Divides*, 179–82. For this section of his work, Putman relies on Bryan Frances as one of his primary sources; Frances, *Disagreement*.

21. Putman, *When Doctrine Divides*, 187.

are not the ones in the best interpretive position, we must decide whether to adopt the opposing stance or suspend our judgement temporarily until we can be better informed.[22] Pastors many times fall in the trap of people's expectations: they come with questions, pastors should have answers. But pastors in contemporary times must understand they simply cannot be informed about everything. Sometimes the best pastoral answer is "I do not know" or "I am not sure"; a pastoral heart is more interested in the flock's health than in nurturing a false ego.

In fact, pastors recognize the wolf metaphor is applied to leaders. In the communities represented in Isaiah and John, the problem was located within the institutionalized leadership; therefore, pastors should never be quick to assume it is others who are the problem. A pastoral heart is aware that even "sound doctrine" driven by an unhealthy ego can be more damaging than false teaching because the harm it causes will distance the sheep from further seeking the truth in the church context.

Dealing with a plethora of interpretations is something pastors should make peace with. McGrath states that if Scripture holds the highest authority, Protestantism "is obliged to recognize that multiple interpretations of Scripture will ensue, with no authorized means of determining which is 'orthodox' and which 'heretical.' This difficulty can be alleviated, but not resolved."[23] Here lies the importance of tradition, an inheritance which Latin American Pentecostalism has neglected.[24] If the Spirit is as powerful as Pentecostalism preaches, then we must humbly recognize he has never stopped moving among his church. Tradition can be Spirit-infused. Creedal faith formation must be reclaimed at local Latin American Pentecostal churches.

---

22. Putman, *When Doctrine Divides*, 193.

23. McGrath, *Heresy*, 217.

24. On a personal note, while growing up in a Latin American Pentecostal church I was never taught a single creed. I realize this may sound unbelievable to most people from other traditions. The contents of the creeds were something one absorbed through general formation, but not explicitly learned as a formula.

How Might We Respond?

The Pentecostal theologian James K. A. Smith denounces that the postmodern idea of a "religion without the religion" is nothing but a continuation of modern sensibilities that seek the assurance of knowing before venturing into believing. The church, in contrast, understands it deals with the realm of mysteries and responds with faith: "the proclamation and adoption of 'thick' confessional identities. . . . [A] Radical Orthodoxy."[25] I dare to speak from my experience when I say new generations of Latin American Pentecostals are deconstructing their faith in search of these thick confessional identities, identities they are unable to find in their local churches.

Of course, this does not completely resolve the matter of differing interpretations but provides a "playing field" for healthy faith exploration. Pastors are the ones responsible for the task of proving that orthodoxy can be "imaginatively compelling, emotionally engaging, aesthetically enhancing, and personally liberating"[26] in the local church context.

The Challenge of Relational Faith

A second challenge pastors deal with is the relational nature of faith. Suspicious postures assume the creeds are the result of power games won by an elite that sought to crush dissenting ideas, but these really should be understood as the result of a productive conflict that seriously weighted all available options. The resulting creeds represent the *consensus fidelium*, the consensus of the faithful.[27] The Bible attests about itself that it is a book written by a community of faith, for a community of faith; Christian faith rightly understood can never be individualistic. While belief is cognitive, faith is relational in nature. Faith is primarily about "trust, commitment, and love. . . . [While] beliefs [embodied by

---

25. Smith, *Who's Afraid of Postmodernism*, 117.
26. McGrath, *Heresy*, 234.
27. McGrath, *Heresy*, 27–28.

creeds] represent an attempt to put into words the substance of that faith."[28]

The relational nature of truth is stressed by Downing: "The most significant postmodern thinkers acknowledge that truth is relational as well: it is perceived through the beliefs, values and practices of the community."[29] To think that humans are able to live without external, social determination is nothing but a modern myth. Willimon points us to the reality that it is not a matter of *if* we are determined by a community of interpretation but *which* community of interpretation we are allowing to determine our lives.[30] His warning to pastoral leaders who are dealing with questions about their faith is noteworthy and relevant:

> It is fair to have a lover's quarrel with the tradition of the church, to wrestle with and to question which tradition is sanctioned by God and which is spurious irrelevancy. Yet it is not fair to place oneself or one's culture above the story of Jesus of Nazareth as represented in the creeds, councils, and faith of the church.[31]

Pastors develop deep relationships with the Good Shepherd and his flock, both the immediate manifestation of this flock in the local church as well as the *historical flock* over which other ministers have presided. Nurturing these contemporary and historical relationships sustains ministry.

The Purpose behind Divine Destruction

In my opinion, there is a difference between *divine deconstruction and renewal of faith* and other kinds of deconstruction of faith. Isaiah 29:13 shows the destruction God is bringing to his people's wisdom and thought structures comes with the explicit purpose of drawing their hearts closer to him. This distinction is important

---

28. McGrath, *Heresy*, 22.
29. Downing, *How Postmodernism Serves (My) Faith*, 206.
30. Willimon, *Pastor*, 19–20.
31. Willimon, *Pastor*, 22.

How Might We Respond?

because some kinds of deconstruction *can* produce the opposite effect: draw people away from God.[32]

Look at Peter's experience long before coming to the house of Cornelius, while he was still walking with the incarnated Christ. As the crucifixion approached, Jesus announced some startling news to his disciples: "Simon, Simon, Satan has asked to sift all of you as wheat. But I have prayed for you, Simon, that your faith may not fail. And when you have turned back, strengthen your brothers" (Luke 22:31–32 NIV). Simon's faith was about to be torn to the ground. What is astounding about this announcement is that the agent this time was not the Holy Spirit but Satan. Even more shocking is the fact that God allowed it. Jesus' warning shows this event was very serious, Peter's faith could in fact fail, and all Jesus could do was pray. Nevertheless, if Peter did come back after going through this soul-crushing experience, he would be in the position of strengthening other people's faith.

Three lessons come to mind when reading this passage.

1. **Trust and Patience.** Deconstruction of faith has a mystery to it. There are times in which people need to be left alone to face the mystery. The only way for a pastor to know when to step back and when to insist is by cultivating a sensibility to the voice of the Spirit and a meaningful relationship with the person going through deconstruction. Swoboda warns that patient reflection is so uncomfortable that we sacrifice it at the altar of quick fixes and responses, and when we do "we assume a compassionate God is obliged to alleviate suffering instantaneously,"[33] so we do the same when helping others by hastily giving them memorized responses. But the author reminds us how Jesus did not deal with Thomas's doubts until a week later. Even more important, during that time of doubt the apostle was still a significant part of the community of faith.

---

32. Deconstruction of faith can also lead people away from the church body, while they are still earnestly seeking for God.
33. Swoboda, *After Doubt*, 113.

2. **Prayer and Second Chances.** Pastors acknowledge that not everything is solved by a sermon and very little is accomplished by asserting one's authority, yet they understand a prayerful pastoral heart can accomplish great victories. A heart like this prepares a leader to welcome back someone into the community of disciples, not only without judgement, but even encouraging them to continue walking into God-given purposes stronger than ever. God honors a pastoral heart.

3. **God's Redeeming Power.** Not every deconstructive process might be led by the Spirit, but even those events led by the adversary can yield fruit for the kingdom of God.

God leads his people into destruction and renewal of their faith with the main purpose of drawing them closer to him; he did it to the community found in Isaiah, but also to the community in Corinth.

The Blessings for the Community in Corinth

The second instance in which God states he is going to destroy and renew human wisdom can be found in the first letter to the church in Corinth: "As God says in the Scriptures, 'I will destroy the wisdom of all who claim to be wise. I will confuse those who think they know so much'" (1 Cor 1:19 CEV).

This citation is one of "the twin pillars upon which Paul's exposition is being constructed [1:19 and 1:31] . . . taken from passages that depict God as one who acts to judge and save his people in ways that defy human expectation."[34] These are used in a context in which fascination with leadership skills and knowledge started breaking the community into different factions. It must be noted that such leaders did possess outstanding skills and knowledge, yet the attitudes springing from the community in Corinth did not necessarily reflect the behavior modeled by the leaders these factions were formed after (Paul, Cephas, and Apollos). There was even a Christ-faction: people probably claiming to be the real

---

34. Hays, *First Corinthians*, 26.

How Might We Respond?

followers of Christ while simultaneously failing to reflect the attitudes of Christ. The Spirit-filled, tongues-speaking Corinthian community was in urgent need of a deconstructive work by the Spirit that allowed the body to be healed by God's saving actions.

The mention of what Jews and Greeks are after is used to represent not only what the Corinthian church was admiring, but these served to epitomize "the basic idolatries of humanity.... For both of these the ultimate idolatry is that of insisting that God conform to our own prior views as to how 'the God who makes sense' ought to do things."[35] As a response to these idolatries in the Corinthian church, the cross is presented as an epistemological revolution, one that introduced a paradoxical worldview in which the greatest power and wisdom the world has ever encountered was shown through the weakness and folly of a cross.[36] Only the cross could tear down the gods raised up by human wisdom, gods that were nothing but "a projection of human fallenness and a source of human pride... [gods that made] considerable demands on the ability of people to understand them... [becoming] gods only for the elite and 'deserving.'"[37]

The cross was the unequivocal fulfillment of the promise of divine destruction of our human wisdom and expectations. The Scriptures were the place this promise was found. Paul introduces the words of Isaiah with the use of his absolute γέγραπται (*gegraptai*), a formula he uses exclusively to refer to the Hebrew Bible; "for Paul to say 'for it is written' is sufficient argument."[38] Thiselton quotes Ulrich Luz at this point: "For Paul, the OT is not in the first place something to understand, but it itself creates understanding."[39] Divine destruction and renewal of faith for the Corinthian church happens when the Scriptures are taken seriously and used to interpret God's saving actions.

---

35. Fee, *First Epistle to the Corinthians*, 77.
36. Hays, *First Corinthians*, 27.
37. Hays, *First Corinthians*, 76.
38. Hays, *First Corinthians*, 72.
39. Thiselton, *First Epistle to the Corinthians*, 160. He cites from Luz, *Das Geschichtsverständis des Paulus*, 134.

Deconstruction and the Spirit

The destruction the Corinthian church is facing is explained by Thiselton: "God chose to reverse what was perceived as wise in an event which appeared to consist in weakness and failure, but would lead in the longer term to new beginnings and to a chastened, transformed, people."[40] This is a great description of how many believers experience deconstruction, what appeared to be a failure caused by weak faith, ends up being a transformational new beginning.

For a community about to experience a new beginning by God's transformational work, the Lord provided several blessings.

The Blessing of a Pastoral Heart

The Corinthian correspondence exhibits Paul's pastoral heart. It is easy to think about the apostle solely as a great theologian; after all, the term "pastor" occurs once in the *Corpus Paulinum*,[41] yet his letters are explicitly pastoral, even if Paul never applies such a title to himself.[42]

By reading 2 Cor 11, we realize it is Paul's pastoral heart towards the church in Corinth that makes him endure the hardships of ministry and what ultimately proves his apostleship. The authority to speak over the lives of the Corinthian church does not come simply from position, but from a *proven* pastoral heart. This heart is put in stark contrast to a false apostle's heart, an image that comes close to that of the wolf and the thief. A few aspects that prove a pastoral heart are devoted presence, personal sacrifice, commitment, attention, patience, and time. A false pastoral heart, a wolf-heart, would exhibit the opposite attitudes.

One of the key factors of having a pastoral heart is the way in which ministry is exercised. Beasley-Murray notes how Paul's tone becomes parental when he writes about Onesimus or to the Corinthian church, something he avoids when writing to Rome or

---

40. Thiselton, *First Epistle to the Corinthians*, 161.
41. Beasley-Murray, "Pastor, Paul As," 654.
42. Wilkins, "Pastoral Theology," 877.

How Might We Respond?

Colossae, churches he did not establish. The parent-child metaphor was widely used in the ancient world to describe a master-disciple relationship. Paul presents himself both as mother and father (1 Thess 2:7-8; 11:12; Gal 4:19-20; 1 Cor 3:1-3; 4:14-21), calling his children to imitate him, not as an act of arrogance, but because of a close pastoral relationship that involved encouragement and discipline. It is dangerous to mistake the parent-child metaphor of leadership as an excuse to infantilize believers. By doing so we run the risk of becoming authoritarian tyrants or micromanagers of the flock. None of these postures reflect the character of the Good Shepherd. On the contrary, Paul limited his own authority to appealing and encouraging instead of commanding. His pastoral heart taught the churches how to make their own decisions by giving them space, time, and arguments; this is the kind of leadership God provides for a community facing a divine destruction and renewal of their faith.[43]

We can see why it would be a mistake to sever a relationship with this kind of leader. Even so, the Corinthian church was favoring the many voices of other teachers (1 Cor 4:15). A leader who fears losing a person's heart to dangerous voices might be tempted to assume an authoritative role over that life, but it would only make things worse. Paul presents us with a wise approach that requires the patience of a pastor, not the results or strategies of a manager.

The Blessing of Mystery

The second blessing God provided for the community of Corinth was the gift of mystery, but not in the way they expected it. Senkbeil claims the core of pastoral character or temperament (*habitus*) revolves around mystery, i.e., stewarding the central mystery of God, which is Jesus. In his opinion, if our ministry revolves around the idea of a spiritual message, we betray our calling by becoming salesmen for the gospel, "always scrambling to persuade reluctant

---

43. Some examples cited by Beasly-Murray showing Paul's nonauthoritative style are Rom 12:1; 15:30; 16:7; 1 Cor 1:10; 4:16; 16:16; Eph 4:1; 1 Thess 2:11. Beasley-Murray, "Pastor, Paul As," 654-57.

customers to buy our product, rather than serving as emissaries sent by God to issue his perennial joyous invitation toward genuine freedom and release: 'Repent and believe the good news' (Mark 1:15)."[44] Senkbeil defines mystery as "something beyond the reach of human sensory perception and intellect,"[45] but through Christ, the inaccessible mystery that is God revealed itself to humanity. Hence Paul's understanding of ministry is explained to the Corinthians as those who are "servants of Christ and as those entrusted with the mysteries God has revealed" (1 Cor 4:1 NIV).

Thiselton acknowledges two problems regarding the word *mystery*. For modern readers, "*mystery* tends to convey what is impenetrable not because it necessitates revelation but because it can never in principle become coherent or intelligible . . . [while for those Corinthians seduced by the appeal of mystery religions] the word would signify a knowledge shared exclusively by 'insiders.'"[46] Neither the modern nor the Corinthian concept of mystery is what Paul intends; he explains to the Corinthians that God's wisdom is the revealed mystery of the crucified Christ: "God's wisdom is not some inaccessible teaching spoken in secret. . . . 'Mystery' ordinarily refers to something formerly hidden in God from *all* human eyes but now revealed in history through Christ and made understandable to his people through the Spirit."[47]

Zahnd calls the church to approach faith with the perspective of a mystic, who is "a person who seeks and at some level attains *a direct experience within the mystery of God*."[48] Following this definition, some mystics found in the Bible would be Abraham, Jacob, Moses, David, Elijah, Mary the Mother of Jesus, Peter, John, Mary Magdalene, and Paul.[49] From a Pentecostal perspective, all these examples and the promise of Pentecost in which the Spirit filled

---

44. Senkbeil, *Care of Souls*, 29.
45. Senkbeil, *Care of Souls*, 20.
46. Thiselton, *First Epistle to the Corinthians*, 241.
47. Fee, *First Epistle to the Corinthians*, 112.
48. Zahnd, *When Everything's On Fire*, 125.
49. Zahnd, *When Everything's On Fire*, 129–30.

everyone at the Upper Room means that every believer is invited into the life of a mystic, into the revealed mysteries of God.

Now, a mystery revealed is not a tamed enigma. The problem with some of the Corinthian believers was their attitude of superiority which led them to consider the message of the cross as milk for infants, while they longed for the deeper mysteries fit for the mature.[50] This mature/infant imagery may sound similar to Paul's parent/child metaphor, but the way some of the Corinthians were using it differed greatly from Paul's use: *it lacked love*. Those deemed by the Corinthians as novices were treated in a derogatory manner. Therefore, the apostle uses the "strategy of ironic reversal," using their own language against them in the first chapters of the letter, as a way to call the Corinthians back to the wisdom of the cross.[51]

Pastors are stewards of the biggest mysteries in creation: faith, hope, forgiveness, love, redemption, and many others. Yes, the great mystery of God has been revealed through Jesus, but pastors understand mysteries demand one to approach them with supreme reverence, in fear and trembling because "Scripture beckons us toward a world where there is mystery; something is afoot that cannot be contained within our systems of knowledge. . . . Scripture engenders interpretive humility."[52] Humility, born out of love and wonder, is the result of encountering the mystery of a crucified Lord. A humble heart is a prerequisite for something as marvelous as pastoral ministry.

The Blessing of Wise and Loving Boundary Setting

Another blessing God provides to the Corinthian community in need of destruction and renewal of faith is boundaries. Interestingly, the Corinthian church did not have any problems setting boundaries among themselves: they made clear distinctions

---

50. Fee, *First Epistle to the Corinthians*, 109.
51. Hays, *First Corinthians*, 41–42.
52. Willimon, *Pastor*, 117.

between the mature and the novice, those of Paul and those of Apollos, and those who had food and those who lacked it. But they had serious problems setting boundaries between their faith identity and the world around them. The same can happen in communities where deconstruction of faith is taking place. Divisive lines can be drawn between those who are deconstructing and those who are not. These limits can be put in place either by those deconstructing or by those who are not. In other instances, the church has assumed such a defensive attitude toward the world that people who are deconstructing overreact to restrictive rules by completely blurring important limits.

Early Christian communities were searching for boundaries through open dialogue and by sharing foundational documents, but the expansion of the faith and an increasingly antagonistic environment led to a point in which these "communities were simply not in the position to enforce conformity."[53] This led to uncertainty about which resources should be regarded as authoritative, divergent interpretations, and a diversity of worship patterns appeared. However, "the sociological diversity of early Christianity was not matched by anything even remotely approaching theological anarchy,"[54] and as soon as it was possible, the church elaborated formal doctrinal statements to preserve "the central mysteries at the heart of the Christian faith and life while allowing them to be examined and explored in depth."[55]

Deconstruction resists the idea of boundaries because of their tendency to isolate and harm others. Exclusion is something that certainly needs to be avoided, especially in the church context, yet the reality is that every human organization requires boundaries to ensure survival otherwise it would die by dissolution. But boundaries can also kill by isolation, by completely cutting an organization away from the surrounding culture, hence making it irrelevant and cultlike.

---

53. McGrath, *Heresy*, 44.
54. McGrath, *Heresy*, 45–46.
55. McGrath, *Heresy*, 29.

How Might We Respond?

In *The Boundaryless Organization* the authors propose a solution to this challenge by comparing organizations not to lifeless and rigid constructions but to living and adapting organisms. Cells need structure and protection, but if they isolate themselves completely from the surrounding context, they die by the lack of oxygen and nutrients. Nature solved this problem with a divine idea: membranes. Membranes provide the cell with definition and protection, but because they are *permeable*, they allow the cell to access vital nutrients and oxygen. For human organizations "the challenge is to find the right balance, to determine how permeable to make boundaries and where to place them."[56]

The apostle Paul shows how this permeability in the church should be exercised through the interaction of *wisdom* and *love*, not through fixed policies. He clearly condemns the actions of the church member who is having an improper relationship with his stepmother; he also reprehends the use the church has been giving to the arbitration system of pagan magistrates; but he also allows for permeability, "for certain crossing of boundaries, and in both directions."[57] Examples of this approach include allowing a wife to live with an unbelieving husband or to divorce him, welcoming outsiders into the Christian assembly, and believers being able to accept dinner invitations from unbelievers even if it involved eating something that was dedicated to an idol.

This permeability is displayed in Paul's impressive pastoral ability. Even when he is dealing with sensitive issues he clearly distinguishes between *commands, concessions*, and *personal opinions* (1 Cor 7:6, 25). Healthy leadership is always aware of such distinctions, while understanding healthy boundaries are permeable.

Faith leaders have the tendency of paying more attention to the clarity of a boundary than to its healthiness. Some helpful parameters to consider in setting healthy boundaries can be found in what follows.

---

56. Ashkenas et al., *Boundaryless Organization*, 3–4.
57. Furnish, *Theology of the First Letter*, 52–53.

The Centered Set Church

In setting healthy boundaries, the work of theologian Mark Baker can be very helpful. He is no stranger to the challenge boundary-making presents for faith communities: he brings together his experience as a missionary in Tegucigalpa, Honduras, with Paul Hiebert's approach on bounded and centered sets to differentiate between bounded churches, fuzzy churches, and centered churches.[58]

Bounded Churches. Bounded churches are those which draw lines to differentiate outsiders from insiders. The line divides correct beliefs and behaviors from incorrect ones. Those who do not meet certain criteria are excluded, which yields feelings of inferiority on them, meanwhile insiders tend to be self-righteous. The problem is not in having clear boundaries itself; the issue is that these boundaries are enforced by shaming and excluding.

Fuzzy Churches. Fuzzy churches solve the line-drawing problem by completely erasing the lines. This approach resonates with postmodern sensibilities that champion tolerance as a supreme virtue. Distinction is vague, and membership cannot be clearly established. Even when there is much talk about love, this is superficial since truth is sacrificed at the altar of tolerance. The center ends up being the individualistic self, and lives drift aimlessly in relativism. Instead of experiencing faithful pastoral ministry, people are neglected by the pastor's lack of clarity because of the minister's fear of hurting their feelings.

Centered Churches. Unlike fuzzy churches, centered churches can distinguish who is part of the community by putting God at the center and understanding conversion as movement. These churches are more interested in the direction in which a person's life is moving relative to Christ, regardless of how close to the center a person might be. Centered churches are conscious

---

58. Baker, *Centered-Set Church*, 19–41. See Hiebert, *Anthropological Reflections on Missiological Issues*, 107–36. Michael Frost and Alan Hirsch used the exact same concept in their book *The Shaping of Things to Come: Innovation and Mission for the 21st-Century Church*. The concept of bounded sets and churches is also addressed in *Missional Church: A Vision for the Sending of the Church in North America*, edited by Darrell L. Guder.

How Might We Respond?

of the fact that every individual moves at a different pace someone at the margins might be moving faster towards the center than a person who is closer to the center.

The centered church is an attempt to hold high expectations for a discipleship process while simultaneously allowing for high inclusivity. The center, of course, is a construction constituted by the community's understanding of the biblical text, models of discipleship, and the theological traditions that define the community. From a postmodern perspective, defining the center is valid since "truth is situated in contexts," i.e., within a community's perspective.[59] Furthermore, it is logical that "every movement based on core ideas or values has to determine its center on the one hand and its boundaries on the other. What is the focus of the movement? And what are the limits of diversity within the movement?"[60]

The centered church model has its limitations, as any model does. Applying it does not automatically eradicate a bounded church mentality, nor does it guarantee freedom from the challenge of people's sensibilities. Nevertheless, it can be very useful for a church that is genuinely working to find new approaches to faithful ministry in their context.

Doctrinal Taxonomies

To avoid falling into theological minimalism (fuzzy churches) and theological maximalism (bounded churches), Putman suggests the use of doctrinal taxonomies, the sorting or ranking of doctrinal beliefs. This is an attempt to follow the wisdom found in the adage *in necessariis unitas, in non necessariis libertas, in omnibus caritas* (in essentials unity, in nonessentials liberty, in all things charity). *In essentials unity* refers to the beliefs necessary to be called a Christian such as the resurrection of Jesus Christ.[61] *In*

---

59. Downing, *How Postmodernism Serves (My) Faith*, 220.

60. McGrath, *Heresy*, 33.

61. It is worth mentioning that an increasing number of people self-identified as Christians do not believe in the literal resurrection of Christ. A BBC article serves as an example; see "Resurrection Did Not Happen."

Deconstruction and the Spirit

nonessentials liberty recognizes there are things in which no consensus has been achieved between the different church traditions (for example speaking in tongues). *In all things charity* is the declaration that Christian relationships are characterized by love, even when conflicts arise.[62] This principle reminds us that faith is not only a matter of *what* we believe, but of *how* we believe.

Doctrinal taxonomies usually take the form of three circles successively surrounding each other, with the one at the center being the most important. Tony Scarcello suggests the first circle to be *the essentials*, the second circle to be *dogma* (topics heavily affirmed and embraced), and the third circle to be *opinions* held loosely.[63] Wittmer proposes that the central circle be what Christians *must believe*, the following what Christians *must not reject*, and the third what Christians *should believe*.[64] Albert Mohler also suggests theological doctrines comprised of the essentials of Christian faith should be located at the first-level, at the second-level doctrines that generate significant boundaries among Christians, and at the third level doctrines that being minor do not really separate believers even in the same faith community.[65]

Paul's pastoral approach of *commandments, concessions,* and *opinions* could be seen as the practical application of a similar method. This practical wisdom can be very helpful in dealing with deconstruction on a communal level.

How to Believe: Love

"Knowledge puffs up while love builds up" (1 Cor 8:1 NIV). This simple principle attests to the importance Paul gave to *how* Christians believe. Christians in general, whether they are experiencing deconstruction of their faith or not, are prone to mistake knowledge itself as enough for Christian life. Conversations around

---

62. Putman, *When Doctrine Divides*, 214.
63. Scarcello, *Regenerate*, 129.
64. Wittmer, *Don't Stop Believing*, 43.
65. Mohler, "Call for Theological Triage."

How Might We Respond?

deconstruction of faith can become unfruitful intellectual discussions focused on the "right" knowledge. As demonstrated above, what we believe is important, but the Bible calls us to pay attention to *how* we believe, too.

Deconstruction thrives on tensions; it does not rush to solve them. Love is the ultimate tension generator because it fosters deep connections with others. Maly finds the Corinthians to be "fixated with 'individual edification' (*Erbauung*) as against 'corporate construction' (*Aufbau*) of the whole church together."[66] While a loving search for understanding builds others and oneself, an individualistic search for knowledge has terrible consequences. It not simply offends but destroys others; this is Paul's ultimate concern (1 Cor 8:11).[67] Their knowledge and actions regarding food consumption does not affect their relationship with God at all, but it does affect their relationship with their brothers and sisters. The seriousness with which Paul deals with this might be repelled by modern individualistic worldviews.

Conversations around deconstruction of faith need to be reframed and treated under different standards than just knowledge, not as a form of gaslighting and avoiding hard conversations, but out of a genuine understanding that "knowledge is defective if it fails to build up the community in love."[68] The faith others hold is to be regarded as holy and is only to be approached with a loving heart; there is no true discipleship without love.

The tension love creates, where deconstruction thrives, involves finding the balance between self-assertion and community edification; it demands self-imposing limits while using knowledge to build others up. Practical examples in churches might revolve around things like listening to secular music, different theories of atonement, the church and culture, creation care, eschatology, differentiating yoga as an exercise from a form of spirituality, gender issues, the literality of hell, and alcohol consumption. The words of Hays are remarkable: "1 Corinthians 8 must be read as a

66. Maly, *Mündige Gemeinde*, 101.
67. Hays, *First Corinthians*, 142.
68. Hays, *First Corinthians*, 137.

compelling invitation to the 'strong' Corinthians to come over and join Paul at the table with the weak."[69] Only love can build a table robust and big enough where knowledge can be served even if it is not shared by all and love itself is also the main course.

The Blessing of One Body

The imagery of a table of love leads us to the famous metaphor of the body. This metaphor found in 1 Corinthians harmonizes with the Johannine imagery of the vine, which suggests an ecclesiology "based squarely on the concept of unity among believers and with Christ."[70] The Corinthian letter expands the ecclesiology of unity to an ecclesiology of *diversity in unity*.[71] The dissimilarities in the church need not lead to division. There is an interdependent relationship that produces an understanding of one's pain as everyone's pain and one's honor as everyone's honor.[72] No member is able to thrive without the other. This truth is not lived in an esoteric fashion in which the church is seen as an unintelligible group of isolated individuals. The body dynamic manifests itself in daily communion and personal contact with one another's gifts.

How this community looks like might be similar to Balswick et al.'s theory of *The Reciprocating Self*: "the reciprocating self is the self that in all its uniqueness and fullness of being engages fully in relationship with another in all its particularity.... Where distinction and unity are experienced simultaneously."[73] For these authors, a trinitarian perspective entails that "the purpose in life is to be in a reciprocating relationship with God and others"[74] in which a mature person has "the capacity and inclination to reciprocate each of these characteristics: 'to love and be loved, to

---

69. Hays, *First Corinthians*, 142.
70. Smith, *Theology of the Gospel*, 152.
71. Fee, *First Epistle to the Corinthians*, 666.
72. Hays, *First Corinthians*, 216.
73. Balswick et al., *Reciprocating Self*, 54.
74. Balswick et al., *Reciprocating Self*, 334.

forgive and be forgiven, to empower and be empowered, and to know and to be known.'"[75] For these authors the goal of a maturation process is to develop a *differentiated faith*. This is the kind of faith found in the middle of two extremes: an *enmeshed unity* in which singularity disappears, and a *detached uniqueness* in which individuality is overstated.[76]

Both unity *and* diversity are the marks of a healthy church by New Testament standards. Life in such a community is filled with challenges, tensions, and miracles. Perhaps, what might seem like a threat can lead to a faith community that fully enjoys God's provision for those who are facing the unknown.

Conclusion, the Pragmatic Task

An important part of being a leader is running experiments. Not every strategy will be successful, which is why pastors must hold loosely to them, having the wisdom to know when to insist and when to desist. Lartey proposes a pastoral cycle that constantly moves from *experience*, to *exploration*, to *reflection*, to *response*, and finally to *new experience*.[77] This never-ending cycle demands constant brainstorming, implementation, and learning. A strategy that does not work is not harmful if expectations are managed, consequences are measured, and egos are healthy. Pastors should not blindly run after change, they should change things for the sake of growth and maturity.

A pastoral heart that engages in the pragmatic task cultivates a life of servant leadership. The strategies born of a servant leader's heart will in return help the congregation "to change in ways that more fully embody the servanthood of Christ."[78] Dare I say, the ultimate characteristic of Christ's servant heart is *kenotic love*.

---

75. Balswick et al., *Reciprocating Self*, 351.
76. Balswick et al., *Reciprocating Self*, 333–35.
77. Lartey, *Pastoral Theology*, 84.
78. Osmer, *Practical Theology*, 192.

A Word of Advice

THE WISE WORDS OF Qoheleth are extremely relevant for pastoral ministry today: "Do not say, 'Why were the old days better than these days?' For it is not wise to ask that" (Eccl 7:10 NIV). Pastoral ministry has been challenging in every age the church has gone through; but it is *today*, in postmodern times, when the Lord has appointed *us* as pastors. Postmodernity and deconstruction are just another challenge in the long history of pastoral ministry. Pastors should follow the wisdom of the ancient teacher of Ecclesiastes and not invest their energy yearning for that which once was; instead, they should try to faithfully discern what the Spirit is doing in the present, so they can follow him while teaching others to do it as well.

Deconstruction is something that happens, it happens from the inside, it is not a method, it is call, it is a yes to the other, and it is affirmative of institutions. These six characteristics can help pastors care for people in their congregations who are going through deconstructive processes. Moreover, it is my hope that these six characteristics of deconstruction can help pastors cultivate deconstructive processes as part of the work of discipleship, understanding that the church is the best place where divine destruction and renewal of faith, as a work of the Spirit, should happen. It is the transformational work of the Spirit through the Scriptures, the believing community, and mystical experiences with God that pastors crave and not deconstruction itself.

A Word of Advice

I would never pretend this work to be the final word on such a complex topic, but I do hope the present book can facilitate the pastoral work on a key issue. It is my opinion that the Pentecostal tradition is uniquely positioned to deal with deconstructive processes and that people with genuine pastoral hearts can have a deep, positive impact in the lives of contemporary disciples. We look to future in hope.

May God grant us his wisdom and heart. Amen.

Bibliography

Albrecht, Daniel E., and Evan B. Howard. "Pentecostal Spirituality." In *The Cambridge Companion to Pentecostalism*, edited by Cecil M. Robeck Jr. and Amos Yong, 235–53. Cambridge Companions to Religion. Cambridge: Cambridge University Press, 2014.

Archer, Kenneth J. *A Pentecostal Hermeneutic for the Twenty-First Century: Spirit, Scripture, Community.* New York: T&T Clark, 2004.

Ashkenas, Ron, et al. *The Boundaryless Organization: Breaking the Chains of Organizational Structure.* San Francisco: Jossey-Bass, 2002.

Baker, Mark D. *Centered-Set Church: Discipleship and Community Without Judgmentalism.* Downers Grove, IL: InterVarsity, 2021.

Balswick, Jack O., et al. *The Reciprocating Self: Human Development in Theological Perspective.* Downers Grove, IL: InterVarsity, 2016.

Barreto, Raimundo C. "Decoloniality and Interculturality in World Christianity: A Latin American Perspective." In *World Christianity: Methodological Considerations*, edited by Martha Frederiks and Dorottya Nagy, 65–91. Leiden: Brill, 2021. http://www.jstor.org/stable/10.1163/j.ctv1sr6jvr.7.

Beasley-Murray, P. "Pastor, Paul As." In *Dictionary of Paul and His Letters*, edited by Gerald F. Hawthorne et al., 654–58. Downers Grove, IL: InterVarsity, 1993.

Borg, Marcus J. *Convictions: How I Learned What Matters Most.* New York: HarperOne, 2014

Campbell, Heidi A. "Relationship between Religion Online and Offline." *Journal of the American Academy of Religion*, 80.1 (March 2012) 64–93.

Caputo, John D. *Cross and Cosmos: A Theology of Difficult Glory.* Bloomington: Indiana University Press, 2019.

———. *Deconstruction in a Nutshell: A Conversation with Jacques Derrida.* New York: Fordham University Press, 2021.

———. *The Folly of God: A Theology of the Unconditional.* Salem, OR: Polebridge, 2016.

Bibliography

———. *Hoping against Hope: Confessions of a Postmodern Pilgrim.* Minneapolis: Fortress, 2015.

———. "Teaching the Event: Deconstruction, Hauntology, and the Scene of Pedagogy." In *The Pedagogics of Unlearning,* edited by Éamonn Dunne and Aidan Seery. Earth, Milky Way: Punctum, 2016.

———. *What Would Jesus Deconstruct? The Good News of Postmodernity for the Church.* Grand Rapids: Baker Academic, 2007.

Castelo, Daniel, and Kimberly G. Castelo. "Caring for Contemporary Mystics: Pentecostalism and the Mystical Worldview." *Journal of Spiritual Formation and Soul Care* 13.1 (2020) 102–14.

Cheong, Pauline Hope. "Authority." In *Digital Religion: Understanding Religious Practice in New Media Worlds,* edited by Heidi A. Campbell, 72–87. New York: Routledge, 2013.

"Costa Rica." UNESCO, 2018. https://en.unesco.org/countries/costa-rica.

Crouch, Andy. *Playing God: Redeeming the Gift of Power.* Downers Grove, IL: InterVarsity, 2013.

Crowe, Benjamin D. *Heidegger's Religious Origins: Destruction and Authenticity.* Indiana Series in the Philosophy of Religion. Bloomington: Indiana University Press, 2006.

Cummings, Ryan. "You Are Your Memories." YouTube, Nov 4, 2016. https://www.youtube.com/watch?v=s--bdwJ6oKs.

Davis, Ellen F. *Biblical Prophecy: Perspectives for Christian Theology, Discipleship, and Ministry.* Interpretation: Resources for the Use of Scripture in the Church. Louisville: Westminster John Knox, 2014.

Derrida, Jacques. "Force of Law: The 'Mystical Foundations of Authority.'" In *Acts of Religion,* edited by Gil Anikjar, translated by Mary Quaintance. 230–98. New York: Routledge, 2002.

———. *The Other Heading: Reflections on Today's Europe.* Translated by Pascale-Anne Brault and Michael Naas. Bloomington: Indiana University Press, 1995.

———. *Points de Suspension: Entretiens.* Edited by Elisabeth Weber. Paris: Galilée, 1992.

———. *Positions.* Translated by Alan Bass. New York: Continuum, 2002.

———. *Rogues: Two Essays on Reason.* Translated by Pascale-Anne Brault and Michael Naas. Stanford: Stanford University Press, 2005.

Derrida, Jacques, and Geoffrey Bennington. "Circumfession." In *Jacques Derrida,* translated by Geoffrey Bennington. Chicago: University of Chicago Press, 1993.

Derrida, Jacques, and Gil Anidjar. "Of Hospitality." In *Acts of Religion,* edited by Gil Anikjar, translated by Mary Quaintance. 356–420. New York: Routledge, 2002.

Detweiler, Craig. *iGods: How Technology Shapes Our Spiritual and Social Lives.* Grand Rapids: Brazos, 2013.

Doehring, Carrie. *The Practice of Pastoral Care, Revised and Expanded Edition: A Postmodern Approach.* Louisville: Presbyterian, 2015.

Bibliography

Downing, Crystal L. *How Postmodernism Serves (My) Faith: Questioning Truth in Language, Philosophy and Art.* Downers Grove, IL: InterVarsity, 2006.

Dussel, Enrique. "The Epistemological Decolonization of Theology." In *Concilium 2013/2: Postcolonial Theology*, edited by Hille Haker et al., 21–31. London: SCM, 2013.

Enns, Peter. *The Sin of Certainty: Why God Desires Our Trust More Than Our "Correct" Beliefs.* New York: HarperCollins, 2016.

Escobar, Samuel. *The New Global Mission: The Gospel from Everywhere to Everywhere.* Downers Grove, IL: InterVarsity, 2003.

"Estas Serán las Grandes Tendencias de Redes Sociales en el 2022." Revista Summa, Nov 16, 2021. https://revistasumma.com/estas-seran-las-grandes-tendencias-de-redes-sociales-en-el-2022/.

Fee, Gordon D. *The First Epistle to the Corinthians Revised Edition.* The New International Commentary on the New Testament. Grand Rapids, MI: Eerdmans, 2014.

Fernández Guardia, Ricardo. *Historia de Costa Rica: El Descubrimiento y la Conquista.* San José, Costa Rica: Librería Lehman & CIA., 1941.

Fowler, James. *Stages of Faith: The Psychology of Human Development and the Quest for Meaning.* New York: HarperCollins, 1995.

Frances, Bryan. *Disagreement.* Malden, MA: Polity, 2014.

Frost, Michael, and Alan Hirsch. *The Shaping of Things to Come: Innovation and Mission for the 21st-Century Church.* Grand Rapids: Baker, 2003.

Fuentes Belgrave, Laura. "Cambios en las Creencias Religiosas en Costa Rica." *SIWÔ* 9.1 (2015) 51–77. http://dx.doi.org/10.15359/siwo.9-1.3.

Furnish, Victor Paul. *The Theology of the First Letter to the Corinthians.* New Testament Theology. Cambridge: Cambridge University Press, 1999.

Gadamer, Hans-Georg. *Truth and Method.* 2nd ed. Translated by Joel Weinsheimer and Donald G. Marshall. New York: Crossroad, 2004.

Goldingay, John. *The Theology of the Book of Isaiah.* Downers Grove, IL: InterVarsity, 2014.

González, Justo L. *Santa Biblia: The Bible Through Hispanic Eyes.* Nashville: Abingdon, 1996.

González, Ondina E., and Justo L. González. *Christianity in Latin America: A History.* Cambridge: Cambridge University Press, 2008.

Gorman, Michael J. "The Interpretation of the Bible in Protestant Churches." In *Scripture: An Ecumenical Introduction to the Bible and Its Interpretation*, edited by Michael J. Gorman, 195–216. Grand Rapids: Baker Academic, 2010.

Green, Joel B. *Body, Soul, and Human Life: The Nature of Humanity in the Bible.* Grand Rapids: Baker Academic, 2008.

Guder, Darrell L., ed. *Missional Church: A Vision for the Sending of the Church in North America.* Grand Rapids: Eerdmans, 1998.

Gulley, Philip. *The Evolution of Faith: How God Is Creating a Better Christianity.* New York: HarperOne, 2011.

Gunter, Nathan H. "For the Flock: Impetus for Shepherd Leadership in John 10." *The Journal of Applied Christian Leadership* 10.1 (Spring 2016) 8–18.

Bibliography

Hanson, Paul D. *Isaiah 40–66*. Interpretation: A Bible Commentary for Teaching and Preaching. Louisville: Westminster John Knox, 1995.

Hastings, Adrian. *A World History of Christianity*. Grand Rapids: Eerdmans, 1999.

Hauerwas, Stanley, and William Willimon. "Embarrassed by God's Presence." *The Christian Century*, Jan 30, 1985, 98–100.

Hays, Richard B. *First Corinthians*. Interpretation: A Bible Commentary for Teaching and Preaching. Louisville: Westminster John Knox, 1997.

———. *The Moral Vision of the New Testament: A Contemporary Introduction to New Testament Ethics*. New York: HarperOne, 1996.

Hiebert, Paul G. *Anthropological Reflections on Missiological Issues*. Grand Rapids: Baker Academic, 1994.

Holland, Clifton L. *Un Análsis de la Obra Evangélica de Costa Rica en 2013–2014 en Perspectiva Histórica*. San Pedro, Costa Rica: Programa Latinoamericano de Estudios Sociorreligiosos PROLADES, 2014. https://www.ranchocolibri.net/prolades/cri-estudio-nacional-2014-final/Un%20Analisis%20de%20la%20Obra%20Evangelica%20en%20Costa%20Rica,%202013-2014.pdf.

———. *Historia de la Iglesia Evangélica Costarricense: Reseñas Históricas Denominacionales*. Guanacaste, Costa Rica: Programa Latinoamericano de Estudios Sociorreligiosos PROLADES, 2017.

———. "Religión en Costa Rica." PROLADES, Jan 25, 2002 http://www.prolades.com/costarica/religion.pdf

Jenkins, Philip. *The Next Christendom: The Coming of Global Christianity*. New York: Oxford University Press, 2011.

Jenson, Robert W. *Systematic Theology: The Triune God*. Vol. 1. New York: Oxford University Press, 1997.

Johnson, D. H. "Shepherd, Sheep." In *Dictionary of Jesus and the Gospels*, edited by Joel B. Green et al., 751–54. Downers Grove, IL: InterVarsity, 1992.

Karris, Mark Gregory. *Religious Refugees: (De)Constructing Toward Spiritual and Emotional Healing*. Orange, California: Quoir, 2020.

Kinnaman, David, and Mark Matlock. *Faith for Exiles: 5 Ways for a New Generation to Follow Jesus in Digital Babylon*. Grand Rapids: Baker, 2019.

Kling, Fritz. *The Meeting of the Waters: 7 Global Currents That Will Propel the Future Church*. Colorado Springs: David C. Cook, 2010.

Langberg, Diane. *Redeeming Power: Understanding Authority and Abuse in the Church*. Grand Rapids: Brazos, 2020.

Lartey, Emmanuel Y. *Pastoral Theology in an Intercultural World*. Eugene, OR: Wipf & Stock, 2006.

———. "Pastoral Theology." In *The Cambridge Dictionary of Christian Theology*, edited by Ian A. McFarlan, 371–73. Cambridge: Cambridge University Press, 2011.

Londoño, Juan Esteban. "Hermenéuticas Postcoloniales." *Alternativas Revista de Análisis y Reflexión Teológica* 22.49 (January-June 2016) 147–64.

Bibliography

Louw, J. P., and Eugene A. Nida, eds. *Greek-English Lexicon of the New Testament: Based on Semantic Domains.* New York: United Bible Societies, 1989.

Luz, Ulrich. *Das Geschichtsverständis des Paulus.* Munich: Kaiser, 1968.

Lyotard, Jean-François. *The Postmodern Condition: A Report on Knowledge.* Translated by Geoff Bennington and Brian Massumi. Minneapolis: University of Minnesota Press, 1984.

Magnin, Lucas. *Cristianismo y Posmodernidad: La Rebelión de los Santos.* Barcelona: CLIE, 2018.

Maly, Karl. *Mündige Gemeinde: Untersuchungen zur Pastoralen Führung des Apostels Paulus im 1. Korintherbrief.* Stuttgarter Biblische Monographien 2. Stuttgart, Germany: Katholisches Bibelwerk, 1967.

McGrath, Alister. *Heresy: A History of Defending the Truth.* New York: HarperOne, 2009.

McKnight, Scot. "Spirituality in a Postmodern Age." *Stone-Campbell Journal* 13 (Fall 2010) 211–24.

McKnight, Scot, and Laura Barringer. *A Church Called Tov: Forming a Goodness Culture That Resists Abuses of Power and Promotes Healing.* Carol Stream, IL: Tyndale, 2020.

McLaren, Brian D. *The Great Spiritual Migration: How the World's Largest Religion is Seeking a Better Way to Be a Christian.* New York: Convergent Books, 2016.

Meyers, Carol. *Rediscovering Eve: Ancient Israelite Women in Context.* New York: Oxford University Press, 2013.

"Migración Neta—Costa Rica." Banco Mundial, 2017. https://datos.bancomundial.org/indicator/SM.POP.NETM?locations=CR&view=map.

Milbank, John. *Theology and Social Theory: Beyond Secular Reason.* Cambridge, MA: Blackwell, 1991.

Milbank, John, et al., eds. *Radical Orthodoxy: A New Theology.* New York: Routledge, 1999.

Mohler, R. Albert., Jr. "A Call for Theological Triage and Christian Maturity." Albert Mohler, Jul 12, 2005. http://www.albertmohler.com/2005/07/12/a-call-for-theological-triage-and-christian-maturity/.

Murillo, Álvaro. "Encuesta CIEP-UCR Evidencia una Costa Rica Estatista y Menos Religiosa." Semanario Universidad, Jul 7, 2021. https://semanariouniversidad.com/pais/encuesta-ciep-ucr-evidencia-a-una-costa-rica-estatista-y-menos-religiosa/.

Murphy, Nancey. *Beyond Liberalism and Fundamentalism: How Modern and Postmodern Philosophy Set the Theological Agenda.* Valley Forge: Trinity Press International, 1996.

Olson, Roger E. *The Journey of Modern Theology: From Reconstruction to Deconstruction.* Downers Grove, IL: InterVarsity, 2013.

Osmer, Richard R. *Practical Theology: An Introduction.* Grand Rapids: Eerdmans, 2008.

Oswalt, John N. *The Book of Isaiah, Chapters 1–39.* The New International Commentary on the Old Testament. Grand Rapids: Eerdmans, 1986.

Bibliography

Padgett, Alan. "Christianity and Postmodernity." *Christian Scholar's Review* 26.2 (Winter 1996) 129–32.

Pargament, Kenneth, et al. "Spirituality: A Pathway to Posttraumatic Growth or Decline?" In *Handbook of Posttraumatic Growth: Research and Practice*, edited by Lawrence G. Calhoun and Richard G. Tedeschi, 121–37. Mahwah, NJ: Erlbaum, 2006.

Peterson, Eugene H. *The Pastor: A Memoir*. New York: HarperCollins, 2011.

———. *Working the Angles: The Shape of Pastoral Integrity*. Grand Rapids: Eerdmans, 1995.

Pontifical Biblical Commission. "Interpretation of the Bible in the Church." Catholic Resources, Jan 6, 1994. Last updated Jul 15, 2006. https://www.catholic-resources.org/ChurchDocs/PBC_Interp-FullText.htm.

Putman, Rhyne R. *When Doctrine Divides the People of God: An Evangelical Approach to Theological Diversity*. Wheaton: Crossway, 2020.

Rainie, Lee, and Barry Wellman. *Networked: The New Social Operating System*. Cambridge, MA: MIT Press, 2012.

"Resurrection Did Not Happen, Say Quarter of Christians." BBC, Apr 9, 2017. https://www.bbc.com/news/uk-england-39153121.

Robinson, Brett T. *Appletopia: Media Technology and the Religious Imagination of Steve Jobs*. Waco, TX: Baylor University Press, 2013.

Rohr, Richard. *The Universal Christ: How a Forgotten Reality Can Change Everything We See, Hope For, and Believe*. New York: Penguin, 2019.

Root, Andrew. *The Pastor in a Secular Age: Ministry to People Who No Longer Need a God*. Grand Rapids: Baker Academic, 2019.

Roxburgh, Alan J. *Missional Map-Making: Skills for Leading in Times of Transition*. San Francisco: Jossey-Bass, 2010.

Scarcello, Tony. *Regenerate: Following Jesus After Deconstruction*. Eugene, OR: Wipf & Stock, 2020.

Scheuerman, William. "Globalization." Stanford Encyclopedia of Philosophy Archive, 2023. https://plato.stanford.edu/archives/spr2023/entries/globalization/.

Seitz, Christopher R. *Isaiah 1–39*. Interpretation: A Bible Commentary for Teaching and Preaching. Louisville: Westminster John Knox, 1993.

Senkbeil, Harold L. *The Care of Souls: Cultivating a Pastor's Heart*. Bellingham, WA: Lexham, 2019.

Sloyan, Gerard. *John*. Interpretation: A Bible Commentary for Teaching and Preaching. Atlanta: Westminster John Knox, 1988.

Smith, D. Moody. *The Theology of the Gospel of John*. New Testament Theology. New York: Cambridge University Press, 1995.

Smith, James K. A. *Thinking in Tongues: Pentecostal Contributions to Christian Philosophy*. Grand Rapids: Eerdmans, 2010.

———. *Who's Afraid of Postmodernism: Taking Derrida, Lyotard, and Foucault to Church*. Grand Rapids: Baker Academic, 2006.

Stofanik, Stefan. "Introduction to the Thinking of John Caputo: Religion without Religion is the Way out of Religion." In *Between Philosophy and Theology:*

Bibliography

Contemporary Interpretations of Christianity, edited by Christophe Brabant and Lieven Boeve, 19–25. Farnham, England: Routledge, 2010.

Sutton, Matthew Avery. "The Day Christian Fundamentalism Was Born: How a Meeting in Philadelphia Changed American Religion Forever." *New York Times*, May 25, 2019. https://www.nytimes.com/2019/05/25/opinion/the-day-christian-fundamentalism-was-born.html.

Suurmond, Jean-Jacques. *Word and Spirit at Play*. Grand Rapids: Eermans, 1994.

Swoboda, A. J. *After Doubt: How to Question Your Faith without Losing It*. Grand Rapids: Brazos, 2021.

Tamez, Elsa. "Lectura Latinoamericana y Caribeña de la Biblia y Lectura Postcolonial de la Biblia: Una Comparación Crítica." *Revista Bíblica* 82.1–2 (2020) 167–88. https://www-digitaliapublishing-com.fuller.idm.oclc.org/a/68582.

Taylor, Mark C. *Erring: A Postmodern A/Theology*. Chicago: University of Chicago Press, 1984.

Tetlow, Joseph A. "Discernment in a Nutshell." Ignatian Spirituality. https://www.ignatianspirituality.com/making-good-decisions/discernment-of-spirits/discernment-in-a-nutshell/.

Thiselton, Anthony C. *The First Epistle to the Corinthians*. The New International Greek Testament Commentary. Grand Rapids: Eerdmans, 2000.

Tillich, Paul. *Shaking of the Foundations*. New York: Charles Scribner's Sons, 1948.

Um, Stephen T., and Justin Buzzard. *Why Cities Matter: To God, the Culture, and the Church*. Wheaton: Crossway, 2013.

Vanhoozer, Kevin J. *The Cambridge Companion to Postmodern Theology*. Cambridge: Cambridge University Press, 2003.

Volf, Miroslav. *A Public Faith: How Followers of Christ Should Serve the Common Good*. Grand Rapids: Brazos, 2011.

Volf, Miroslav, and Matthew Croasmun. *For the Life of the World: Theology That Makes a Difference*. Grand Rapids: Brazos, 2019.

Wariboko, Nimi. *The Pentecostal Principle: Ethical Methodology in New Spirit*. Grand Rapids: Eerdmans, 2012.

Wariboko, Nimi, and Amos Yong. *Paul Tillich and Pentecostal Theology: Spiritual Presence and Spiritual Power*. Bloomington: Indiana University Press, 2015.

Watkin, Christopher. *Great Thinkers: Jacques Derrida*. Phillipsburg, NJ: P&R, 2017.

Westphal, Merold. *Whose Community? Which Interpretation? (The Church and Postmodern Culture): Philosophical Hermeneutics for the Church*. Grand Rapids: Baker Academic, 2009.

Wilk, Florian. "Isaiah in 1 and 2 Corinthians." In *Isaiah in the New Testament: The New Testament and the Scriptures of Israel*, edited by Steve Moyise and Maarten J. J. Menken, 133–58. London: Bloomsbury, 2005.

Bibliography

Wilkins, M. J. "Pastoral Theology." In *Dictionary of Latter New Testament and Its Developments*, edited by Ralph P. Martin and Peter H. Davids, 876–82. Downers Grove, IL: InterVarsity, 1997.

Willimon, William H. *Acts: Interpretation; A Bible Commentary for Teaching and Preaching*. Louisville: Westminster John Knox, 2010.

———. *Pastor: The Theology and Practice of Ordained Ministry*. Nashville: Abingdon, 2016.

Witherup, Ronald D. "The Interpretation of the Bible in the Roman Catholic Church and the Orthodox Churches." In *Scripture: An Ecumenical Introduction to the Bible and Its Interpretation*, edited by Michael J. Gorman, 195–216. Grand Rapids: Baker Academic, 2010.

Wittmer, Michael E. *Don't Stop Believing: Why Living Like Jesus Is Not Enough*. Grand Rapids: Zondervan, 2008.

Woodward, James, and Stephen Pattison. *The Blackwell Reader in Pastoral and Practical Theology*. Malden, MA: Blackwell, 2000.

Yoder, Amzie. "Fundamentalism and the Church in Central America." *Mission Focus* 2 (1994) 45–50.

Zahnd, Brian. *When Everything Is on Fire: Faith Forged from the Ashes*. Downers Grove, IL: InterVarsity, 2021.

www.ingramcontent.com/pod-product-compliance
Lightning Source LLC
Chambersburg PA
CBHW071441160426
43195CB00013B/1995